PRAISE

Observations *of* an A

and a Mindf

"A lovely memoir, as clean and fresh as the stream the Farmer brings to life."

—Allen Appel, author of the *Alex Balfour* series

"In this dazzling display of erudition and adventure, Harry Kavros traces his meditative journey from urbanite professional in NYC to neophyte farmer in NC. Local farmers and newfound neighbors share domestic wisdom that makes his vast literary repertoire take on fresh meaning. A consummate storyteller offers a tale to ponder and treasure."

—Bruce B. Lawrence, Marcus Family Humanities Professor of Religion Emeritus, Duke University

"In loving detail, Harry Kavros shares the story of his departure from the ivory tower and reconfirms that, even in this hyper-technological age, Nature remains the most essential metaphor for the human experience. He gives us a Romance in which the hero adventures in an exotic landscape, confronting all manner of creatures and defending the virtue of the ideas and the aesthetics he holds dear. This book is a deeply humanist meditation that connects him (and us) to centuries-old traditions of seeking and finding meaning in the world around us."

—Nathan Kotecki, author of *My Love for You Will Still Be Strong*

"Seeded with the works of literary giants, Kavros's thought-provoking prose is a reminder that our humanity has always been inextricably connected to and informed by our time in nature."

—Aaron Vandemark, Chief Proprietor and Chef, Hillsborough Bakeshop and Pasta Co. and Panciuto, James Beard Best Chef Southeast Semifinalist 2011–2016, 2022

"After a career in academia, Harry Kavros purchased a small farm in the Piedmont, North Carolina. His unvarnished account of what he has learned from clearing the land, tilling the soil, and raising animals is brimming with insight, laced with humor and humility, and enlivened by fresh readings of western literature."

—Brooks Graebner, Historiographer, The Episcopal Diocese of North Carolina; Rector, St Matthew's Episcopal Church, Hillsborough, NC, 1990–2017

"Harry Kavros has the heart of a storyteller and the intellect of the humanities professor he used to be. As I read this book, frequently on the NYC subway, I was transported to the challenges and beauty of farm life and enjoyed catching up with writers I love through the varied literary references he weaves into his essays."

—Retta Blaney, author of *Working on the Inside: The Spiritual Life Through the Eyes of Actors*

"*Observations of an Accidental Farmer* is a compelling read as a memoir of making the life change from Manhattan to a farm in North Carolina and as a review of related literature. As a psychologist, I appreciate the author's reflective description of the process of growth and change as he moved to farming and living on the land. His extensive knowledge of literature provides us with thought-provoking quotes from a wide range of authors which add depth to the memoir. It is one of the most enjoyable reads I have had in a long time."

—Joan Farrell, Adjunct Faculty in Clinical Psychology, Indiana University-Purdue University Indianapolis; author of *Experiencing Schema Therapy from the Inside Out*

Observations *of* an Accidental Farmer– *and a* Mindful Reader

Observations *of* an Accidental Farmer— *and a* Mindful Reader

HARRY KAVROS

pdb

PAUL DRY BOOKS

Philadelphia 2024

First Paul Dry Books Edition, 2024

Paul Dry Books, Inc.
Philadelphia, Pennsylvania
www.pauldrybooks.com

Illustrations by Schuyler Semenuk

Printed in the United States of America

Library of Congress Control Number: 2024935060

ISBN: 978-1-58988-191-4

for Peri

Whither thou goest, I will go;
and where thou lodgest,
I will lodge.

". . . but tho' an old man, I am but a young gardener."

—Thomas Jefferson to Charles Willson Peale, 20 August 1811

"But what does Socrates say? 'Just as one person delights in improving his farm . . . so I delight in attending to my own improvement day by day.'"

—Epictetus, *Discourses* 3.5.1

"There are spiritual dangers in not owning a farm."

—Aldo Leopold, *A Sand County Almanac*

Contents

Appendix
Authors and Works Mentioned in the Text

Acknowledgments

Peri and I left family and friends behind when we moved to North Carolina. To help keep in touch, I started writing holiday letters, with snippets of farm life. Peri's oldest friend, Kris Linder, suggested that I expand my meditations into a book. Thus began *Observations of an Accidental Farmer.* Allen Appel, local Hillsborough author and friend, read the manuscript and offered much needed encouragement. Miriam Cook, Professor of Arab Cultures, and I spent lovely hours critiquing each other's work. I'm sure I got the better deal, as she nudged me toward making my narrative more personal. My publisher, Paul Dry, saw promise in an early manuscript and introduced me to Ellen Marlene Airgood, a wonderful novelist who improved almost every paragraph. Her red pencil and wisdom made my observations and reflections more readable, intimate, and vivid. Finally, my wife, Peri, saw some value in the project and kept the creative fires stoked. Every page has been inspired by her love and care.

Introduction

*Song of the Open Road**

We looked like a wagon of death. A manual branch trimmer, wedged in diagonally across the back seat of a car laden with luggage, poked its jagged-toothed scythe out the left rear window. The grim reaper rode shotgun, a fitting companion on this journey of ours, for surely it is the knowledge of death that inspires us to make sense of our lives.

The car carried a few essentials—an inflatable mattress, changes of clothing. Incongruously, a set of china colonized much of the back seat and gave us a look of privilege. We lugged these boxes of fragile dishes and accessories in order to sell them at a North Carolina warehouse. The funds would help offset the cost of my parents' assisted living apartment, where we had moved them before allowing ourselves to move. We also transported some of my father's tools, an ironic inheritance as I lacked talent in carpentry or any other manual art. Shovels, hammers, awls, wrenches, and saws crammed every remaining nook.

Seduced by the prospect of life in warmer climes, my wife, Peri, and I left Manhattan. Peri left her psychology practice, and I left my career as a university dean and side gig of literature teacher. During the past couple of years, we had traveled to San Antonio and Boca Raton, to

*Walt Whitman's poem from his 1856 collection *Leaves of Grass*

interviews in Virginia, Georgia, and North Carolina. We had circled Tennessee. Then, in a spur-of-the-moment decision, we put our New York apartment on the market, rented a car, and drove to Hillsborough, North Carolina. There we found a lovely, pine-filled landscape and a small town, replete with Colonial and Civil War history, handsome architecture, and local dives in which laborers and farmers outnumbered financiers and lawyers. On the drive home, we made an offer on a house and heard that a young couple wanted our apartment. We bought and sold over the weekend.

Now, traveling south again to move into our new home, we tried to avoid turnpikes and four-lane divided highways. Our improvised route went through small Delaware towns and Virginia pine-shaded valleys. Most mom-and-pop diners had long since disappeared, and the colonial landscape was dotted with modern chain restaurants. The crisp primary colors of their signs blared against the subtler emeralds and sages of pine groves and fields.

The sides of pickup trucks and vans announced the sort of economic activity we had not witnessed for decades: services for lawn care and septic tanks, stump removal, lawn mower repair, pest control, and water testing. The distances between villages increased the further we traveled, and driving past gas stations without filling the tank became ever riskier.

Stopping for a breakfast of waffles and bacon, we were awed by the ease with which the waitress started a conversation. Hospitality seemed more important than economic exchange. Her openness was contagious, and we in turn explained where we came from and where we were going. The waitress told us about the local ice cream shop, the high school's football team and Halloween parade, and her marriage plans. She had been raised in the village a few miles down the road and had never left the county. This experience was repeated in almost every restaurant, gas station, and hotel on our rambling journey to North Carolina.

I left my last position as dean questioning the values of my university. I left pondering mortality—that of my parents as well as my own. I left New York, my home for three decades, an old man (that is, by Archaic Greek terms—I was older than the middle-aged Odysseus, closer to his elderly father, Laertes). I was not, like Whitman, a new kind of hero of the open road, "afoot and light-hearted,"* wandering wherever I chose. Instead, I left presuming it would be my last major journey. And like Odysseus, perhaps I would find order, homecoming, and respect for the gods. I would synthesize what I'd read and taught with my daily life on the property we'd just purchased.

As Lee Smith's young diary writer, Molly, wrote in *On Agate Hill*, ". . . it is always an adventure, like Gullivers Travels and Robinson Crusoe and the Odyssey. All the books are about somebody going someplace." The young Molly, a survivor of the Civil War, Reconstruction, and rape, learned that there are many other journeys. There are psychological journeys, spiritual journeys, political journeys, journeys through history and fantasy worlds, theological journeys, as well as road trips. My own road trip from New York to below the Mason-Dixon line, and

*From Whitman's "Song of the Open Road"

my adventures on the farm, would include these different journeys.

We named our property Hyacinth Farm. Hyacinth is a Cretan name ("inth" is a typical Minoan suffix, as in labyrinth) for a mythological young man, beautiful and beloved of Apollo. Unfortunately, he died when trying to catch a discus. I came to learn that death and beauty mingled on the farm as in Greek myth. Apollo made a flower from the dead lad's spilled blood, and his tears stained the petals with the sign of his grief. Peri would soon plant several hundred hyacinth bulbs around the property. As for the farm, we would start with seventeen guinea fowl, fifteen exotic chickens, and a dog that romped among, and occasionally attacked, the birds. Peri imagined pastures filled with peacocks, sheep, and goats. A horse rambled in a lovely front acre. A retired stallion, Oliver, literally had been let out to pasture. I would soon feel his pain.

To be clear: I am not a farmer. I did not move south to live simply or deliberately. I did not intend to discover the joy of wiggling my fingers through rich dirt. Nor is my livelihood dependent upon agriculture or livestock. I do not intend to insult real farmers by comparing my novice attempts to plant seeds or raise chickens with theirs. I did not even intend to purchase acres of woods and pastures. When I did, I wanted to make the landscape wondrous and the land productive. But what I found was gnarled underbrush, fallen trees and branches, a clogged creek, barren pastures, and untended weeds. Although racoons, snakes, and coyotes visited, the only permanent inhabitants were chiggers and ticks.

The Landscape

Hydraulic Systems

For two weeks, we lived in a house furnished only with an inflatable bed, waiting for the furniture and kitchen implements to arrive. Built in the early 1950s by a lumber baron, each room hosted his prized woods. Mahogany, cedar, knotty pine, oak, and redwood surrounded us. The house, covered with old-fashioned cedar shakes, resembles a long, one-story cabin. I was determined to avoid steps, thinking of weak knees in the not-distant future.

Once we unboxed the pots and the books and arranged the chairs and the bed, we began to explore the property. Our twenty-two acres had dozens of nooks and crannies, and despite the long trip we were anxious to get to know them. Tangled brambles and the blanket of fallen branches hindered our footsteps and required negotiating with rocks, holes, and slippery Japanese stiltgrass. I recall the grandmother's advice in Annette Clapsaddle's novel *Even as We Breathe*: "Keep your head down in the woods."

This invasive Asian species, also called Nepalese browntop, crossed the Pacific Ocean as packing material in the early twentieth century. It appears initially as a lovely, pillowy garden ornament, but quickly springs up calf-high and overtakes woods and pastures. It is easy to uproot, but virtually impossible to eradicate. Botanists, state park rangers, and frustrated neighbors all told me the only remedy is burning every stalk and seed every season for seven consecutive years.

More disturbing, for me, was the decrepit state of a creek whose shores meandered from a lake on a neighbor's property through ours and finally through a large cement pipe running underground to the property across the road. The creek bed was littered with muck (a rich and decaying mixture of leaves and mud) and rocks. Plus, the owners of the lake had capped an overflow pipe that would have fed the creek.

A decayed wooden bench on the shore suggested that a previous owner had meditated on this view, which once must have seemed majestic. Now, rusted metal fencing, a sluggish creek, and woods choked with weeds proved how quickly a landscape can collapse into chaos. The law of entropy is remorseless and brutal. I slowly made my way upwards toward the house, depressed by the prospect of hundreds of hours of labor to reverse the damage.

In the course of the next several months, I worked to simplify the landscape and remove the rot that had intruded upon it. I uprooted and hauled away hundreds of feet of rusted wire squares topped with barbed wire. Over the past few generations, new tree growth had encircled the fence and earth had buried its lower quadrants. Even after months of labor with shovels and wire cutters and shoulders, remnants remain, entangled among old roots and clay and protected by bark for future landowners to discover.

Removing rotting fences allowed the landscape to flow. We had a wider expanse of trees and enjoyed picturesque views of woods rolling into pastures. Partially satisfied, I began work on the creek to achieve what Olmsted considered the triumvirate of elements of landscape design: woods, pasture, and water all merging seamlessly.

Reading Olmsted on landscape design, I realized where some of my melancholy gets its drive. A clogged landscape or woods fallen into disrepair causes anxiety. The destruction of the garden has bothered a host of American writers. For Thoreau, the intrusion of the railroad into the woods portended the end of pioneer innocence and the beginning of our bondage to machines, strict schedules, and an oppressive economic system. Similarly, the hapless granddaughter in Flannery O'Connor's "A View of the Woods" lamented the building of a gas station, which destroyed her pastoral view and any breathing space in her constricted life.

Flowing water rivals lapping flames in its ability to keep our eyes fixated. Wading through the creek seemed like a charming stroll through shimmering eddies, until a rubber boot sank knee deep into the depthless muck. Water rushing into my boot created a powerful suction force, and coated my foot and leg with ooze and made me suspicious of Thoreau's innocent pleasure in creek-walking, recorded in his *Journal*:

> . . . the attractiveness of a brook depends much on the character of its bottom. I love just now to see one flowing through soft sand like this, where it wears a deep but irregular channel, now wider and shallower with distinct ripple-marks, now shelving off suddenly to indistinct depths, meandering as much up and down as from side to side, deep-

> est where narrowest, and ever gullying under this bank or that, its bottom lifted up to one side or the other, the current inclining to one side.

I began by shoveling mud from heavily silted areas and hurling heavy loads of muck yards inland and uphill far enough so heavy rains could not slide them back. Once or twice a long black snake, until then watching me unnoticed, lunged into the stream and remained hidden beneath the murky water. For several days I dredged the creek uphill toward the lake, and for several more downhill toward the road. The entire slope could not have been more than a few feet, but as Thoreau wrote in *A Week on the Concord and Merrimack Rivers*, only a fraction of an inch is sufficient for water to flow.

My mind did not drift, as Thoreau's did, to heroes of former wars, even though Nathaniel Greene fought major battles of the Revolutionary War's Southern campaign at nearby Guilford and from there marched through the state to final victory at Yorktown. I was more sympathetic to his musings about the common people who farmed the area until only a couple of generations ago, the unheard and unrecorded folk whom the poet Thomas Gray called mute inglorious Miltons.

As I worked, I was burdened by thoughts of futility. I would spend hours moving rocks of all sizes from the creek bed. I lined the shore with them to release water pressure and keep dirt from eroding into the creek. But I knew the creek would eventually move even the largest rock and carve steeper curves out of the shore. Nonetheless I continued, hoping that one day soon a rapidly flowing creek would be more attractive.

But tree branches and trunks continued to fall over the creek. As I budged some and chain sawed others, the water began to flow. I found it remarkable how much that movement allowed the maple trees and the oaks to come into focus. Once I detected a current, I forgot the sweat streaming from my brows and the paralysis of my wrists and hands. I pulled the hoe out of the creek bed and leaned on the handle. For a moment weariness emptied my mind, which quickly started wandering. This small stream invited meditation—on time, on mortality, on nature's power and our Lilliputian stature.

I also pondered the long journey of each single drop of water and the relentless force of myriads of drops. Two sources feed the creek that meanders through our property. The permanent source is the lake that overflows through a neighbor's pipe into the ditch that becomes the creek. During thunderstorms, torrents of water carve additional pathways to the creek. Over just the last century, a golf course, country roads, and houses have been built around the creek, which leads to the Eno River, then into the Neuse River, then into the Atlantic Ocean.

Tracing the water's path into ever-widening perspectives reminds me of the startling passage in the "Ithaca" chapter of *Ulysses*, in which water from Leopold Bloom's kitchen tap is said to flow from "ocean flowing rivers with their tributaries and transoceanic currents: gulfstream, north and south equatorial courses: its violence in seaquakes, waterspouts, artesian wells, eruptions, torrents, eddies, freshets, spates, groundswells, watersheds, waterpartings, geysers, cataracts, whirlpools, maelstroms, inundations, deluges, cloudbursts," and ultimately into the county reservoir, a "subterranean aqueduct," and Dublin water mains.

By now I have returned to the old bench, and I imagined a former inhabitant meditating at the creek during a leisurely moment. My own mind meanders whenever I'm not working with dangerous tools or pushing my muscles to their limit. Peering over the bench to the wooded slope on the other side of the creek, my thoughts started to flow. This is how my days proceed: one observation (or sound, or smell) triggers musings on topics historical, philosophical, and literary.

Or memories. As I paused my exertions at the creek, I scanned the past decades. During the last decade of my thirty years in Manhattan, I was a university dean. To keep a smattering of sanity, I had teaching gigs on the side. At Columbia, I taught in the great books seminars, nicknamed lit-hum, that had remarkably survived tumultuous curriculum changes for almost a century. For six years I read and re-read Homer's *Iliad* and *Odyssey,* Greek playwrights and historians, *Genesis,* Augustine's *Confessions* and Dante's *Inferno,* Montaigne's essays, *Don Quixote, Crime and Punishment, Pride and Prejudice,* and *To the Lighthouse.*

At Fordham I taught a variety of books, including *Gilgamesh, The Hobbit,* and *Moby-Dick.* When I was a dean at the business school, I created a course on business in American literature, in which we mused on what Ben Franklin's *Autobiography,* William Dean Howell's *Silas Lapham,* or Sinclair Lewis's *Babbitt* could teach us about the various stages of capitalism.

Throughout my farming experience, the books I had taught and the questions my students asked remained obsessively in my head. Great writers are so adept at unsettling readers that it's difficult to escape their gravitational pull. My attempts to capture an urban professor's experience on the farm never entirely pulled free from literary or philosophical meditations. In the short essays that follow, ordinary and mundane moments inspired me to think about Odysseus or a philosophical problem or a historical crisis.

Now, staring at the creek I had just dredged, my mind wandered to past centuries, when a Native tribe dwelled along this minor tributary. The Occaneechi tribe flourished in the area until European explorers arrived. Those explorers and the settlers who followed, who would soon disrupt the tribe's peaceful existence, envied their communal organization and trade routes. In 1701 John Lawson encountered one of their villages near Hillsborough. He was treated hospitably, but secretly recorded evidence of their prosperity:

> About Three a Clock, we reach'd the Town, and the Indians presently brought us good fat Bear, and Venison, which was very acceptable at that time. Their Cabins were hung with a good sort of Tapestry, as fat Bear, and barbakued or dried Venison; no Indians having greater Plenty of Provisions than these. The Savages do, indeed, still possess the Flower of Carolina, the English, enjoying only the Fag-end of that fine Country.*

The Occaneechi controlled trading paths that connected Virginia through North Carolina to the interior

*John Lawson published *A New Voyage to Carolina* in 1709.

of North America. In 1676 the tribe had fought alongside Nathaniel Bacon against other Native tribes in Virginia. Occaneechi warriors captured a Susquehannock fort, but the British demanded all the spoils (mainly furs). Though their first battle was a stalemate, the English killed the tribe's chief, Posseclay, and over one hundred men, women, and children.

"Wherever I go," wrote Thoreau in his *Journal*, "I tread in the tracks of the Indian." It is easy to forget, while sauntering in the woods, choked with awe at the sight of towering pines, that native tribes hunted and planted here. It is the final blow of civilization when tribal names survive mainly on street signs, and when we have forgotten the human history of the forests.

Back at the creek, I sat precariously on the edge of the old bench. Its boards having rotted over dozens of winters, it was not sturdy enough to support me. I easily stomped the seat and the arms into small planks, which I burned in one of the fireplaces.

The prospect of the massive effort ahead of me to clear the land and subdue the stubborn Japanese stiltgrass lay heavily on my mind. But on my way back to the house, my arms laden with wooden remains, I could hear the creek flowing behind me.

Greek Lessons

In Autumn, gravity loosened nuts from their branches. Hickory nuts carpeted our pastures. They were large enough to welt the skin and scalp when they plummeted from towering branches. Oaks are even more prolific. During mast years, when weather, genetics, and resources converge to produce a massive harvest, I have seen sheets of acorns raining to the ground. Our largest oak, which looms over our house, has a girth of over twelve feet at its base. Peri and I together can barely wrap our arms around it. A botanist told me that in a good season this tree alone produces over ten thousand acorns, a crop I measure by the wheelbarrow load as I rake and scoop and trundle them away from our doorstep. I gather that the oak is playing the odds—only one seed in one million will survive into treehood.

It is impossible to walk near oaks without treading on—and more often rolling on—swaths of acorns. The word *acre* is related to the Old English word for acorn, and for a plot of land with oak trees on it. Oaks and their acorns were especially important to medieval pig farmers, who needed the right to "acker" pigs on unenclosed lands in order to fatten them. I have no pigs, but deer and squirrels abound. I consider these woodland creatures a great resource, as they can reduce an acre of slippery nuts into scattered emptied hemispheres as they forage and store food for the winter.

Native Americans made better use of oaks than I can. They used their nuts for lamp oil and their trunks for canoes. They also kept healthy during winter months by chewing on pine and other evergreen trees. The molecular chemistry that supports this natural wisdom is mapped out in David George Haskell's *The Forest Unseen*. The sun's rays transfer energy to the electrons in chlorophyll. This captured energy is used to create sugar in plant cells. In winter the food-making process hibernates, leaving the energy in the electrons without their typical outlet. Haskell writes that trees

> prepare for winter by stocking their cells with chemicals that intercept and neutralize the unwanted electron energy. We know these chemicals as vitamins, particularly vitamins C and E. Native Americans also knew this effect and chewed winter evergreens to keep healthy through the winter.

As for the rest of the trees, they shed hundreds of branches over the autumn months, or whenever they cannot resist the force of ice or fierce winds. Every spring I push my wheelbarrow around each pasture, collecting fallen limbs and dumping them into heaps that look like giant beaver dams. Lots of folks around here do controlled burns, and the odor of burning leaves and cedar often wafts through the woods. Some neighbors surreptitiously grow hemp, and smoke from those fields smells like the hallways of my college dorm. I swear that's why Gibbs, our first rescue Doberman, sometimes seems high.

After my first spring, I decided to try to reduce one of my own heaps of branches to ashes. The pile I chose was a few yards from the tree line, so I thought it was safe enough. Nonetheless, I connected several hoses to reach the spot, which I turned on when the flames quickly engulfed the tinder. When the bonfire reached a dozen feet upwards, it scarred a few nearby pines. I hosed the surrounding grass and nearby barks, but the heat was so ferocious that I had to retreat. The air seemed to wave; everything seemed fuzzy. When I took off my glasses to wipe my forehead, I saw that the glass lenses had begun to melt. Tucking the ruined spectacles in my pocket, I considered wood-chipping for the next pile.

The most dramatic instance of nature succumbing to gravity occurred while Peri walked Gibbs and Danni (our second rescue Doberman) in one of the pastures, shortly after my experiment with fire. Since this pasture's metal fence had been battered by years of falling branches, Peri stayed close to the dog to keep him from leaping across the creek and into the woods in one direction or through the woods and onto the street in another. Peri noticed that Gibbs seemed agitated, like a horse dancing nervously as it senses an imminent earthquake. She had started to move homeward when she heard a thunderous cracking sound. She turned her head as a three-story red oak crashed a few yards behind her, slicing an apple tree in half during its descent. The aged oak left a crater by the creek, exposing vast rotted roots.

I hired someone with a 36-inch chain saw to help me clear the pasture of the fallen trunk. He was wiry, and with a broad smile asked if I would like to lift the machine. I yanked it up about a foot, and surely would not have been able to run it with a steady hand. I watched as he wielded a tool that neither my insurance nor my fear of death allowed. Within an hour he had cut the mammoth tree into 18-inch cylinders. Over the next few days, I pushed the cylinders, with the determination of Sisyphus, over the uneven earth toward the edge of the creek.

Heraclitus said, "nature loves to hide." Perhaps instead of a gnomic utterance he should have attempted an observation. He might have said, for example, "nature falls." Even a casual observer in the woods knows that every few minutes a leaf, a nut, a twig, a branch the size of an anaconda, or an entire tree falls to the ground. The larger falling branches are called widow makers. That's how the Argonaut hero Jason died. Elderly, weary, alone, he rested under his old ship Argo when a rotten piece of wood from the ship fell on his head.

The cycle of new growth and falling branches is so common that Darwin incorporated it into one of his most famous similes for natural selection.

> As buds give rise by growth to fresh buds, and these, if vigorous, branch out and overtop on all sides many a feebler branch, so by generation I believe it has been with the great Tree of Life, which fills with its dead and broken branches the crust of the earth, and covers the surface with its ever branching and beautiful ramifications.*

Keats was a bit more maudlin, as he yearned for something more permanent in his apostrophe, "Ah, happy, happy boughs! that cannot shed your leaves, nor ever

*From chapter 4 of Darwin's *On the Origin of Species*

bid the Spring adieu."* Thomas Hardy was sadder still. Before he described the brutal work and savage weather on the farm in "The Farm Woman's Winter," he sighed a hopeless fantasy: "If seasons all were summers, and leaves would never fall . . ."

An aphorism such as "nature falls" might have shifted ancient thinkers from philosophical speculation toward empiricism. Greek philosophers might have been inspired to discover gravity or entropy, and they would have shortened by two millennia the time it took proto-scientists to couple hypothesis with experiment and thus invent the scientific method. Begin with observation, not philosophical speculation. Perhaps this is what Wittgenstein meant when he said, "What is hidden is of no interest to us."†

*From John Keats' poem "Ode on a Grecian Urn"

†Wittgenstein's *Philosophical Investigations*

Bones

Like a child preparing to build a fort, I spent hours collecting fallen trunks and branches. I selected the largest pieces first, dragging them singly across pastures to build a base. I can drag two mid-size pieces, one on each arm. The smaller ones I shlepped into a heap. The resulting structure resembled a malformed geodesic dome, or an apprentice beaver's dam.

I hurled cedar bark onto growing piles of detritus, grateful that my knees, hips, and wrists had thus far held together. After about one year, the land was relatively clear, except for the piles. This activity does not require particular skill, just brute force.

No Tom Sawyer tricked me into this work, only a mysterious internal dynamic. I cannot determine whether the virtue of perseverance or the vice of stubbornness is the driving force. When I'm optimistic I prefer to think that I have the sculptor's ability to see negative space, or what the land might look like when the excess material is removed. When that optimism evaporates, I see only obsessive-compulsive disorder, a phrase often on Peri's lips.

One day, while flinging wood onto a pile behind a towering oak, I noticed a pale white, curved object among the branches. Taking a closer look, I discovered a fibula of an animal larger than a raccoon but smaller than a coyote. Its bleached whiteness gave it an ancient aura, and not for the first time I felt like an intruder in the woods.

Clutching the old bone, I paused for a moment, my spectacles drooping down my nose from sweat and my plaid shirt stretched and stained from nature's detritus. I recalled the path Thoreau's mind traveled at such a moment. When he came upon bleached bones he mused about primitive instincts (like eating a woodchuck raw).*

My mind traveled a much shorter distance, at most a generation or two back. Tobacco and corn were grown in these parts, and pastures hosted cattle and sheep. But however vast the tracks of land were, they rarely competed with the grandeur, productivity, and wealth of the plantations of the Deep South. North Carolina had relatively few land barons, and their plantations required relatively fewer slaves. The lack of aristocracy was one reason the state was famously called a vale of humility between two mountains of conceit. The one grand house with slave quarters in nearby Stagville is a rarity.

Instead of slave labor, farmers around here used primitive methods and their own muscle, guiding plows behind their mules well into the mid-twentieth century. A local tradesman, descendant of a long line of southern farmers, told me his grandparents were sharecroppers just outside of town. Their mule pulled their hand-forged iron plowshare through rigid rows of clay, and a modest yield of tobacco crop maintained their family at a subsistence level. Shoeless younger children attended to the chickens while the older ones helped scatter seed or harvest the crop.

*From the "Higher Laws" chapter of *Walden*

During the Depression, a Durham banker foreclosed on several large farm properties here in Orange County and subsequently carved them into smaller parcels. Our property was once part of such a much larger farm. In a front pasture, closer to the road, there was a small pine cabin, big enough for a Franklin stove, a bed, and a shotgun. I have discovered a couple of partially buried brick foundation posts, and the daffodils that sprout there every February descend from those planted at a front door, where occasional carriages were invited to stop along the road to exchange news.

A couple of decades later, construction of our house began. Many of our magnificent oaks and red maples and hickories were saplings then. The bleached bone I unearthed was likely not fully grown or sinewed. In fact, most of the evidence around me, from fallen branches to rotund trunks to skeletal remains, is scarcely two generations old. Yet the fraction of a moment in geological time the bones represent contains multitudes: wrenching changes in local family history, economic turmoil, and property transfers.

As I carried the animal bone home, Thoreau's somber glimpse into distant human ancestry seemed a philosophical luxury. He performs backwards somersaults over recent generations to meditate on primeval animal instinct. He took his sojourn at Walden Pond only seven years after the Panic of 1837. As Thoreau walked through Concord, where one-third of farmers did not own oxen and over half could not afford a plow, he would have observed the economic and social effects of the depression that followed. He was not kind to the subsistence farmer or the day laborer.

Elizabeth Bennet Falls in Love

At the beginning of our North Carolina adventure, I often gazed out our kitchen window and considered how to begin my attack on nature's uncontrolled growth. In the middle distance, the west pasture hosted a dozen varieties of prickly weeds. A carpet of Japanese stiltgrass had marched down the pasture and captured a tree stump. And straggly bushes hid snakes and blocked all entrances to the neighboring woods and pastures.

The woods below, leading to the creek, bristled with underbrush. New saplings had sprouted wherever seeds fell, and I could navigate only by shouldering my way around them. Dangers lurked everywhere, and I grew dizzy from constantly shifting my gaze. On the ground, fallen trunks and branches conspired to trip anyone who dared cross them. Above, hairy vines dangled from treetops and swung between trees. For a while, I tried to pull these vines, thick as hawser ropes, from their tangled branches. Only later did I discover that they were aged poison ivy vines.

It was difficult to see from one pasture to the next, much less walk through the woods. Cedar trees were especially dangerous, as they remain standing when they perish, and when their branches fall, they leave short spikes behind—ready to impale the hapless wanderer. Upon these spikes farmers used to mount mason jars, inviting the summer sun to sterilize them for jams produced in autumn. Dale Chihuly used the same infrastructure to mount his arabesque glass flutes upon a central core to create his massive chandeliers.

I had not yet purchased chain saws, tractors, branch cutters, or weedwhackers. One day, while I was hacking at undergrowth with my father's seventy-year-old shovel and hedge clippers, I came within a few yards of a massive copperhead that had nestled under one of the larger bushes. I froze with the shovel in mid-air, maintaining that awkward position as the sun moved behind a towering oak. The snake looked elderly and calm. Its skin appeared bunched and wrinkled and its eyes looked drowsy. I may have overestimated the likelihood of a venomous strike. Nevertheless, I held my pose so as not to threaten it and dared not blink. The snake in turn maintained a steady gaze on me, and its voluminous girth emitted confidence. After a few minutes I backed away, never to receive the praise Ántonia lavished on Jim in *My Ántonia,* when Jim slays a massive rattler: "I never know you was so brave, Jim. . . . You is just like big mans; you wait for him lift his head and then you go for him." The next day I cautiously approached the bush, and when I had determined that my enemy had vacated, I eliminated its hiding place

It has taken me about one year to open this pasture and these woods. Clearing the woods eliminated several safety hazards, and might even slow the pace of a fire. But the driving force for me was an old-fashioned aesthetic and moral value. In the country house poems of Ben Jonson, Andrew Marvell, and Alexander Pope, long, uninterrupted views from manors indicated that wealthy landlords had greathearted souls. The English landscape architect Lancelot "Capability" Brown was the creative genius who designed landscapes that surrounded aristocratic mansions. Rocks, trees, and rolling fields were rearranged so that they mingled seamlessly. Suddenly a cluttered and shadowed landscape was infused with space and light. The aim was at once to create a tableau that resembled a painting by Poussin and one that seemed natural. Grounds recreated by Capability Brown were ultimately meant to invite contemplation, presumably of the Enlightenment marriage of reason and nature. And finally, the landscape was arranged so that a framed view would be visible from every window.

My favorite example of an artistic intervention in the landscape, and one designed to offer vast and undisturbed views, is the "ha-ha." This innovation was simply a ditch or a sunken fence. Dug in the middle distance, it created a boundary to a park or garden, preventing cows from crossing without interrupting the view. The ha-ha balances restraint and openness. However silly the name sounds, it is a serious reflection of proper Enlightenment behavior. The merits of such a device, and corresponding morality, are discussed in Jane Austen's *Mansfield Park*.

But in *Pride and Prejudice* the master of the house is revealed as greathearted because of the landscape he has created. When Elizabeth arrives at Pemberley, Fitzwilliam Darcy's country estate, Mrs. Reynolds, the housekeeper, leads her on a tour of the house. Although there are many portraits and sculptures to admire, what strikes Elizabeth most are the vistas. Each window frames a view of an unobstructed, sculptured expanse. The landscape is, in eighteenth-century vocabulary, awful and grotesque—awe-inspiring and grotto-like—

because the landscape artist has made his efforts invisible. The grounds look like nature untouched, but they have been organized from the house outward. Open expanses, clusters of trees, paths around lakes—everything conspires to fill the viewer with moral contemplation. Elizabeth fell in love for several reasons, but what clinched the deal was the revelation that the owner of such a country house, who has organized the contemplative landscape, must be lovable indeed.

I decided to test Austen's insight into the lover's heart and see if I could earn the same response from Peri. After I completed my own landscaping labors, I took Peri for an evening stroll through the newly opened pasture and woods. Her gaze took in the full extent of what months of hand-blistering work had accomplished, and she whispered something about obsessive compulsion disorder. As the setting sun beamed orange through the trees and mottled the leaves, however, Peri stopped mid-sentence, and her quiet smile shone with gratitude.

The Civic Gaze: First Meditation

I began my reading on rural landscape architecture while I was an urbanite. When we lived in Manhattan, our apartment was flanked by Morningside Park and Central Park. The latter is the greatest architectural wonder of New York City. Rocks, trees, roads, bridges, bodies of water, and paths are all part of a vast plan to invite the wanderer to wonder. Here is how Frederick Law Olmsted opens his 1858 *Report* on the project: "The horizon lines of the upper park are bold and sweeping and the slopes have great breadth in almost every aspect in which they may be contemplated." The sentence is breathless as it rushes, with conjunctions and without punctuation, toward Aristotle's major virtue.

> As this character [expanses that invite contemplation] is the highest ideal that can be aimed at for a park under any circumstances, and as it is in most decided contrast to the confined and formal lines of the city, it is desirable to interfere with it, by cross-roads and other constructions, as little as possible. Formal planting and architectural effects, unless on a very grand scale, must be avoided . . .

At first blush this warning seems to harden the contrast between city and nature. Olmsted certainly comments throughout the *Description of a Plan for the Improvement of the Central Park* that the boundary between nature and the urban grid is sometimes sudden, distinct, and harsh, in which case it must be softened or hidden with new plantings. But the city's grid and the varied landscape within the confines of the park share one thing: they are both artificial. The difference is that the avenues and the streets constrict one's view, and the (apparently) natural slopes are designed to allow one's view to roam without interruption. It is important, he writes, to "afford facilities for rest and leisurely contemplation upon the rising ground opposite. . . ." As he later claimed in a report on Yosemite Valley, "it is a scientific fact that the occasional contemplation of natural scenes of an impressive character . . . is favorable to the health and vigor of men."

Further, Olmsted claimed that the government was responsible for funding parks for the common citizen. The reason has nothing to do with fairness, or welfare, or redistribution of income. Rather, it has to do with the civic virtues that underlie the continued existence of the republic. The government has a duty to assure that "enjoyment of the choicest natural scenes in the country and the means of recreation connected with them" be "laid open to the use of the body of the people." If the government did not act, those places would be monopolized by the few and their benefits experienced only by an elite. The establishment of great public grounds was therefore required of a republic that derived its authority from its people. Today parks are part of the civic infrastructure. There is a vital link for Olmsted between leisure and contemplation on the one hand and republican virtue on the other. On these grounds, Olmsted should stand as a founder of the second American Republic along with John Bingham and the creators of the Fourteenth Amendment.

Here is the reason Olmsted offers a brief history of parks in his writings. Parks originally excluded plebeians. They were created for the exclusive enjoyment of the king and nobles. From the Babylonian pleasure grounds of Nebuchadnezzar, who had a picturesque park built to relieve the nostalgia of his Median bride, to the Persian gardens stocked with deer for the king to hunt (the Greeks called this kind of garden a *paradeisos*), to the terraced grounds of Roman country houses, parks were noble territory. No different were the enclosed parks of the Tudor kings. It was not the toppling of kings, however, that opened gardens and landscapes to the middle classes and laborers. Public space was the creation of landscape architects like Olmsted, who identified the conditions for the survival of the republic.

Olmsted read deeply in the landscape architects of the eighteenth and nineteenth centuries, such as William Gilpin and Uvedale Price, who valued gothic and romantic excess. This so-called picturesque style consisted of irregular, rocky grottoes, exotic plants, sudden twists in the paths, abrupt banks, and thickets of trees. But he ultimately returned to an earlier style that valued gently sweeping views, distant vistas, and easy gradations from the house to the garden to natural woods, thickets, and pastures.

This simpler style attracted Lancelot "Capability" Brown. Brown's holy trinity of landscape composition were woods, water, and meadows, each modulating into the other, and all visible from the country home. Of course, Olmsted converted Brown's aristocratic, private garden into public urban space. His revolt, according to Lewis Mumford, was "against the depression and misery of the industrial city." His parks, from Central Park in Manhattan to Prospect Park in Brooklyn to Belle Isle in Detroit, are meant to refresh the mind of the citizen who might be otherwise deadened by the density of the city or the monotony of industrialization. This experience of the citizen is the republican version of Elizabeth gazing into the horizon from the windows of Pemberley.

Dog Days

During my dredging mission, I lifted hundreds of rocks the size of coyote skulls from the creek bed and used them to line the banks. Flowing water had softened the rocks' edges and revealed a shimmering patina of bronze and jade.

Peri had three criteria for purchasing our new home: a fireplace, a pool, and a garden. She got all three. One of the fireplaces is larger than a Manhattan studio apartment. The pool was built in the 1960s when the home was converted into a social club (in a dry county, that was a euphemism for drinking club). "Garden" is a bit of an understatement, as we have twenty-two acres, but Peri claimed a few small plots where she could plant yellow daffodils, pink hyacinths, and orange abelia bushes. When I asked her if she would like the creek rocks to adorn her garden, she fretted about my back but smiled at the prospect of a stone border.

I started the project around 7 a.m. one July morning. Within an hour the sun was so hot that spit dried before it hit the ground. Nevertheless, I continued to roll my wheelbarrow down to the creek, fill it with a dozen rocks, and shove it back uphill over terrain filled with roots and ruts.

After dumping rocks one hundred yards above the creek, I didn't know if I would have the stamina to make several round trips.

On my first lurching trek up from the creek, the wheel stuck in a snake hole (I later found a snake's discarded skin nearby). Despite my desperate grip, the barrow overturned and the rocks spilled and tumbled back down toward the creek. Nature wanted to recover its loss, and I cursed my wasted energy.

I collected my rocks and reloaded them, determined to avoid all obstructions. Gritting my teeth, I hefted the handles again and focused on the wheel, swerving every couple of feet to avoid a hole or root. My eyes burning under the sweat, I recited snatches from a William Carlos Williams poem. The short lyric had always fascinated me. I loved how a machine could organize a landscape and focus your eye on bursts of color that explode when something clear (rain drops) and something white (chickens) magnify its redness:

so much depends
upon

a red wheel
barrow

glazed with rain
water

beside the white
chickens.

A phrase as vague as "so much depends" refuses to measure how many things depend or to what extent. But I feel the poet's exuberance and how deeply the images affect his emotions.

I love how the poet's joy in observation is captured in the enjambments, which keep shifting the images. Our mental picture of a red wheel shifts in the next line to a red wheelbarrow. Then rain becomes rain water, and white becomes white chickens. The poem leaves us with a series of shifting impressionist images. The wheelbarrow has been left in the rain somewhere near the chickens. The beauty of red, clear glaze, and white fill the poet with emotion. There is a hint of work in the background—farm labor and tending chickens—but the poet emphasizes peaceful stillness and the play of color. This is a great deal, but for me so much more depends upon this red wheelbarrow.

As I strain with my rocks, I feel the poet's phrase "so much depends" neglects the person whose labor required the red wheelbarrow. My work on the hillside depended upon this combination of lever and wheel, two simple machines that intensify the power of mere human muscle. My wheelbarrow transformed what might otherwise have been impossible—moving large rocks from a creek one hundred yards uphill—into something doable though heart-stopping. It is a georgic tool that makes possible otherwise backbreaking lifting and transporting—rocks, soil, branches, and even lighter but bulky straw. It is not an insight worth mentioning except for the fact that the poet focuses on the wheelbarrow's image, not on its function.

After a lifetime of reading, my mind oscillates between a poet's and a laborer's view of the landscape. Sometimes these two braid around each other, especially when I mentally recite poems, while shoveling or mowing, to lighten the tedium. But more often there is a divide. Williams may hint at work, but the image of sparkling rain drops against red metal trumps any musing about farm labor.

Wordsworth sparked the Romanticism that prized the poet above the laborer. As he wanders lonely as a cloud through grazing pastures, he is the hero of his journey, not the shepherd and his sheep, as his own imagination negotiates its relationship with nature. His *Guide through the District of the Lakes in the North of England*, a tourist handbook to mountains, groves, and lakes, with occasional Roman and medieval antiquities noted, maintains the same isolated and picturesque detachment to the laborers in the fields. It is this tension upon which James Rebanks remarks in *The Shepherd's Life*, a memoir about a line of family shepherds in England's Lake District.

Wordsworth walked through the district at the turn of the nineteenth century and admired "the perfect Republic of Shepherds and Agriculturalists" who were "humble sons of the hills [and] had a consciousness that the land, which they walked over and tilled, had for more than five hundred years been possessed by men of their name and blood." Rebanks, discarding the romantic imagination for a pragmatic one, wrote about the mundane daily tasks necessary to eke out a living as a shepherd: mending walls, chopping logs, treating lame sheep, worming lambs, hanging gates, trimming sheep feet, cleaning the muck from the tails of ewes and lambs. He doesn't admire the landscape as much as understand its every variation. "I see my world stretched beneath me, the three kinds of farmland that make up our world: inbye (meadow), intake (the lower slopes of the fells which aren't common land because they have been enclosed by walls or fences), and fells." As his memoir ends, he finally relaxed into an idle meditative state, so rare that his dog tried to nudge him into his more typical, compulsive movement and attention to his flock. Rebanks's final burst of lyricism was a paean not to the beauty of the landscape or to the flight of the imagination, but to a way of life that comprises diligence and work.

The thought of Rebanks's dog jolted my own thoughts back to earth, and I stopped reciting Williams's poem. Once I had pushed my wheelbarrow all the way up the hillside and onto level ground, I wound my way around trees and dumped the rocks by Peri's garden. By the time I fitted them like puzzle pieces around the border, I could barely move my arms. My fingers tingled with numbness and my forearms were slack. It would take a day for my muscles to recover. After a shower I measured the effect of the morning's work. My red wheelbarrow had turned pink in the glare of the long summer morning. And I had lost three pounds of sweat.

Four Walks in the Woods

In my first foray into our woods, I took in about a third of our property. I stumbled upon piles of tires with worn treads, a black queen-size metal bedframe, and blue-tinted cement blocks. Poison ivy vines swinging from trees and thorned vines sprouting from the earth ensnared me. Lost amidst thick oak, pine, and maple trunks, I traipsed aimlessly into neighboring properties. It must have been decades since anyone had cleared any brush or fallen branches.

I entered the woods beyond the barn anticipating a pensive walk, but too many dangers lurked for me to lose myself in meditation. Obstacles arose with every step. Snake holes, rocks, roots, vines, and leaf-covered ravines all conspired to twist an ankle or snap a fibula. I kept my head down, my eyes scanning the ground. When Audubon, roving American woodlands in the 1820s, attempted to look upwards in wonder, he was also quickly forced to come down to earth: "would that I could represent to you the dangerous nature of the ground, its oozing, spongy, and miry disposition."*

The forest floor smelled of mortality. Fallen branches, desiccated trunks, layers of oak and maple leaves, rotted acorns and hickory nuts, matted pine needles, shed

*From John Audubon's description of the Ivory-billed Woodpecker in his 1842 *Birds of America*

snake skins, decomposed mushrooms: the air was heavy with decay. Hurricanes had felled societies of pines, whose trunks teemed with beetles and ants performing their roles in the forest ecosystem, gnawing, boring, munching, excavating, and excreting. The pines' peeling bark had rotted into mulch. An occasional monstrous oak or poplar had collapsed with age, from lack of sun above or from lack of nutrients below. Thoreau wrote that a journal is a book that records all your joys and ecstasies. Mine also included the threats and dangers lurking in the woods and the invisible mortal combat behind tree bark and beneath tree root.

As I tried to extricate myself from the woods that day, a voluminous spider's web draped my face and arms. Spiders had spun their dense webs between two trees. Along my route, a dozen yards apart, an endless variety of arachnids waited patiently beside vast webs. There were spiders with small abdomens and long legs and with large abdomens and short legs; spiders the size of pin heads and of hoop earrings; spiders with round and with oval abdomens; black, brown, ash, and white spiders.

Darwin wrote about spiders in *Voyage of the Beagle.* There he marveled that the variety of species among the jumping spiders appeared almost infinite. In time I learned to walk waving a long branch in front of me, lest any one of these hunters, fearless as Lilliputians attacking Gulliver, inject their poison, strong enough to kill a carpenter wasp or to leave a welt the size of a peach on a human. Spiders are super-predators, killing about one and a half trillion pounds of prey annually.

I used to have some sympathy for spiders. As a child, I was enraptured as my sixth-grade teacher read *Char-*

lotte's Web aloud to the class. As an adult, I realized that spiders reduced the population of flying pests. As a researcher, I learned from Peter Wohlleben's wonderful *The Hidden Life of Trees* that arachnids and insects might dream. But now that I am their prey, my sympathy has fizzled.

By the time I returned home that afternoon, I had decided to find guides to lead me through my forest primeval. I asked the patriarch of an extended family across the street to help me locate my boundaries, which had become obscured by decayed fences and fallen trees. Jim was a dozen years my senior, but muscular and deft at navigating the woods. He had helped his father carve out a golf course from a vast tract of land across the street. His son now runs the business, but Jim still spends his days riding tractors, mowers, and woodchippers.

Having played in our woods as a youth, he was as familiar with hidden paths and lurking dangers as Cooper's hero Natty Bumppo. Jim walked quickly in his old haunts, showing me the narrow metal tubes hammered into the ground, partially covered by rotting leaves, which marked the property line. He nodded ahead, past several yards of decrepit wire fencing, toward ribbons tied to a rotting cedar fence post, which marked my southwest corner. Glancing beyond the post, I pointed out several piles of old tires, hidden deep in the woods. A few generations ago, Jim said, his uncle owned a tire store. Business lagged during World War II because of rubber rationing. After the war, he decided to hoard old tires to prepare for the next crisis. As a result, his woods are piled with old car and tractor tires. When you stumble upon a tire, said Jim, you know you've transgressed the property line.

Hearing Jim's history of his family's property made me feel claustrophobic for the first time since we'd settled at Hyacinth Farm. The boundary lines I could now see seemed to press against my lungs. I imagined the firewall, guarded by sword-wielding angels, created to keep Adam and Eve from returning to their garden. It may be that boundaries are part of the curse of the human race, along with hard work and painful childbirth. Thoreau, the least likely American author to feel limited by property lines, spent a lot of time observing them. As a surveyor, he measured property lots, and as a casual walker ("to saunter" was his preferred verb), he marked some of his outings by the piles of rocks that marked the limits of local towns.

Farmers cleared forests here many generations ago, Jim explained, to sow tobacco, corn, rye, and other crops. Long after the farmers had gone, oak and maple seedlings fell into the cleared land and took back the fields. Gradually large branches spread, barring sunlight from the forest floor. But Jim never lost his bearings on our walk that day, and soon guided me back to familiar pastures.

I devoted my next sally into the forest to mapping groups of trees. Most of our woods formed battle lines of pines and oaks. The pines are loblolly, or yellow pine, typical of the South. They were bred to grow quickly, in order to feed the timber and paper industries. They also expire quickly compared to oaks, which are sturdier and thicker as well as longer-lived. The battle of the pines and oaks caught the attention of Thoreau, who gave a talk on the subject to the Middlesex Agricultural Society entitled "The Succession of Forest Trees." He dismissed the popular theory of spontaneous generation, which purported to explain how one species or the other would spring up from barren ground. He asserted instead, unsurprisingly now, that trees came from seeds. In the case of the oak, the acorn never fell far from the parent, although squirrels might more widely distribute them. Birds consumed the fruit of other trees and manured the ground with their seeds. Pine seeds were scattered by the wind. And thus, unexpected patterns of new growth sprang up in the woods.

Over the course of a century, the cover of a fast-growing pine might protect a smaller oak from wind and sleet and then, as it crashes to the forest floor, open the canopy to its firmly grounded neighbor. The forest floor is divided between the materials the oaks and the pines shed. There is the cushioned, textured, and manicured floor of fallen pine needles. And there are the slippery, chaotic, uneven, and sloppy piles of brown oak leaves. "Fallen leaves teach us how to die," said Thoreau. In the *Iliad*, the generations of leaves remind the Trojan warrior Glaukos of the generations of men, a sentiment at odds with the system of ethics that valued warriors who stood out from the multitude.*

Mary Oliver began her series of meditations in *Upstream* with a cryptic pronouncement: "One tree is like another tree, but not too much." I'm not sure where the philosophical line is drawn, as Oliver shifted from

**Iliad,* book 6

the Platonic idea of a tree to something more like Wittgenstein's notion of family resemblance. Tree varieties have much in common, of course, including verticality, root systems that mirror above-ground growth, and organs that use the energy of sunlight to transform carbon dioxide into energy and oxygen. My challenge, conversely, was to drill past philosophical realism. My efforts in forest management and landscape design demanded empiricism and the wit to distinguish the myriad forms and textures of bark and leaves.

So I hired a State Ranger to walk the woods with me to help me identify trees with which I was unfamiliar and to manage the growth of the forest. A few weeks later Clell appeared, clad in pressed green slacks and gray shirt, his trim uniform mocking my torn and stained jeans. As we walked, he told me that pine is the second most populous tree in North Carolina. First is the red maple. According to forestry experts, he explained, the real contest is between the pine and hardwood trees, like the red maple. Pine trees grow quickly and block the sun from more slowly growing trees. They are not sturdy and are more easily snapped by fierce winds. Cut down some of the loblollies, he advised, to open up the canopy and make room for the maples, beeches, walnuts, and poplars. Before I could enact his plan, a tornado snapped or uprooted fully half of the mature trees in our woods.

A dozen pines in the southwest corner of the property, felled by Hurricane Fran twenty years before we arrived, were still lined up in the direction of Fran's 120 mile-per-hour winds. Previous owners of these woods had let the land grow wild. It would take me another year to chain saw fallen trunks, remove standing dead cedars, and thin out young growth Clell had assured me had little chance of survival. Cato the Rustic recommended a religious ritual before undertaking such a large task.

> The following is the Roman formula to be observed in thinning a grove: A pig is to be sacrificed, and the following prayer uttered: "Whether thou be god or goddess to whom this grove is dedicated, as it is thy right to receive a sacrifice of a pig for the thinning of this sacred grove, and to this intent, whether I or one at my bidding do it, may it be rightly done. To this end, in offering this pig to thee I humbly beg that thou wilt be gracious and merciful to me, to my house and household, and to my children."*

Clell found red maples near the creek, along with ironwood trees. The latter are also called muscle wood trees, their smooth trunks resembling the taut sinews of a wrestler. The poplar, or tulip tree, was relatively easy to identify (easy for a forest ranger, frustratingly difficult for me). It is the straightest tree, has a whitish hue, and its large leaf has a concave curve instead of a maple-leaf-like point. No tree has as much vertical energy as the poplar. Beeches have smooth, thick trunks. Hackberry barks resemble high relief sculptures that have eroded and lost their outlines, a Michelangelo's *Battle of the Centaurs* in which it's difficult to tell the Lapiths from the hybrid beasts. Walnut trees have diamond-like striations and symmetrical branches. Sycamore trunks

*From Cato the Rustic's *De Re Rustica*

have thin peeling bark, which reveals smooth green underneath.

Although there are no paths in our woods, Clell confidently strode through the roughly hewn openings between the trees. I, on the other hand, could not walk in the same direction for more than a few yards before stumbling to a halt. Recent sprouts, wild undergrowth, ferns, and vines were all hurdles. Finally, we stopped at an elderly tree, where Clell pointed out how much activity there was on the trunk. Segments of bark were in stages of peeling, as the bark made way for a wider girth. Beetles had bored into the trunk; above that, a lightning strike had left black claw marks.

For the first time I saw black strokes on several trees in the woods, typically on the eastern sides. These trees had survived a few life-threatening bolts of lightning, Clell explained, upon which other disasters followed. First, the surge of electricity damaged the outer growth rings, which transport water from root to branch. Second, a damaged section of bark invited hosts of enemies, including fungus and boring insects. Third, once electricity traveled to the roots it would find its way along the mycelial network that attached one tree to its neighbors. Finally, a fire would have ignited and consumed a good portion of the trunk and branches. After Clell finished his litany of disasters, I touched the blackened oak bark, hoping to absorb some native wisdom.

"All the phenomena of nature," wrote Thoreau, "need to be seen from the point of view of wonder and awe, like lightning."* Blake took a different view and mag-

*From Thoreau's *Journal*

nified the awe at the expense of matter. In a letter to the Reverend John Trusler, he absorbed nature into pure imagination:

> The tree which moves some to tears of joy is in the eyes of others only a green thing which stands in the way. Some see nature all ridicule and deformity, and by these I shall not regulate my proportions; and some scarce see nature at all. But to the eyes of the man of imagination, nature is imagination itself. As a man is, so he sees.

Perhaps it was my imagination, but a mystical feeling seemed to permeate the forest floor, especially when giant gnarled roots twisted away from their trunks. Jim's knowledge of his boyhood playground and Clell's expertise with trees ended above ground. I needed a Virgil to guide me in the underworld of roots. The experts I found were nature writers who had discovered complex subterranean networks that nourished communities of trees. Just below the surface, the soil is laced with strands of fungus and bacteria, which connect vast groupings of trees. This mycelial network nourishes the roots and can transfer nitrogen and other nutrients from a healthy tree to a malnourished one. Also called mycorrhizae, from Greek words meaning fungus root, this network of fungal threads, one hundredth of a millimeter in diameter, offer water and nutrients to tree roots in exchange for carbohydrates. Each cubic inch of mycelium compresses eight miles of fine filaments, which can transmit chemical signals to alert trees to approaching predators, such as viruses and insects.

"Land, then, is not merely soil," wrote Aldo Leopold in *A Sand County Almanac*, "it is a fountain of energy flowing through a circuit of soils, plants, and animals." It is this invisible network, which Suzanne Simard dubbed the "wood wide web," that is threatened by herbicides such as glyphosate.

David George Haskell revealed the underground mystery in *The Forest Unseen*, a book of revelations of nature's microscopic activities. He begins with a sexual metaphor, finding a

> complex mating dance in the rhizosphere. The plants' partners are fungi. . . . Fungal threads cover most of the soil like a subterranean spider web. Some are dusky gray and spread out seemingly at random, coating whatever lies in their path. Others grow their white strands in waving lines, diverging then reuniting like rivers in a delta. Each fungal thread, or hypha, is ten times finer than a root hair.

I reveled in the notion of underground spider webs, imagining a Jules Verne-like journey under the soil that mirrored my first foray into the forest swishing webs away from my face. "Because hyphae are so thin," Haskell continues,

> they can squeeze between microscopic soil particles and penetrate the ground much more effectively than can clumsy roots. A thimbleful of soil may contain a few inches of root hairs but a hundred feet of hyphae, spooled around every fleck of sand or silt. Many of these fungi work alone,

> digesting the decaying remains of leaves and other dead creatures. Some, however, work their way into the rhizosphere and begin a conversation with the root. . . . The fungus and the root greet each other with chemical signals and, if the salutation goes smoothly, the fungus extends its hyphae in readiness for an embrace. In some cases, the plant responds by growing tiny rootlets for the fungi to colonize. . . . The plant supplies the fungus with sugars and other complex molecules; the fungus reciprocates with a flow of minerals, particularly phosphates.

This underground intrigue, invisible to me, I took on scientific faith. As for religious faith, many cultures have located deities and other powers below the soil. The Celts of Ireland believed that one of their tribes, the Tuatha Dé Danann, returned from exile to inhabit the underworld. From there they controlled the fecundity of the land above. The Irish poet John O'Donohue writes in *Anam Cara* that it is simply prudent to believe in the wisdom of the soil.

> On a farm you learn to respect nature, particularly for the wisdom of its dark underworld. When you sow things in the spring, you commit them to the darkness of the soil. The soil does its own work. It is destructive to interfere with the rhythm and wisdom of its darkness.

For the ancient Greeks, dangerous divinities lived beneath their cities. The Furies, carefully renamed The

Kindly Ones, represented anger, homicide, revenge, and other forces that threatened to destroy civilization. They needed to be worshipped to prevent such forces from erupting.

The sound of Clell's voice returned me back to the surface of the earth. He pointed out pollinator blossoms atop a cluster of poplars and masses of mistletoe that hung from the uppermost reaches of oak branches. The intensity of sunlight shifted as my eye wandered up and down the trunks. Large canopies captured most of the sun's rays, with shafts finding their way through to create shifting patterns on the fallen leaves below.

The air shimmered around the tree tops, as moisture on the leaves evaporated. I remembered that Darwin also marveled at how the translucent light shifted at different altitudes. "At the height of a hundred feet," Darwin observed in a Brazilian forest, "the hills were buried in a dense white vapour, which rose like columns of smoke from the most thickly-wooded parts, and especially from the valleys."* Thoreau and Emerson both admired the naturalistic detail of Darwin's prose, but I think they appreciated even more his sense of wonder—at the infinite variety of spiders, the multitude of worms just under the surface of the soil, and the luxuriance of the vegetation. The lush noun "luxuriance" is Darwin's, a reminder that he perused *Paradise Lost* during his voyage and must have loved Milton's description of Eden.

The parasitical mistletoe boasts pride of place in *On the Origin of Species*. In the introduction, Darwin refuted other theories of variation in plant and animal species.

*From Darwin's *The Voyage of the Beagle*

> In the case of mistletoe, which draws its nourishment from certain trees, which has seeds that must be transported by certain birds, and which has flowers with separate sexes absolutely requiring the agency of certain insects to bring pollen from one flower to the other, it is equally preposterous to account for the structure of this parasite, with its relations to several distinct organic beings, by the effects of external conditions, or of habit, or of the volition of the plant itself.

Rootless but attached to towering oaks, mistletoe also garnered the attention of Sir James Frazer, who linked it to divine lightning strikes, the death of the Norse god Balder, and Druidic sacrifice. At the other end of the heroic spectrum, Faulkner's simile compares mistletoe to the treacherous and venal Snopes family: "The Snopes sprang untarnished from a long line of shiftless tenant farmers—a race that is of the land and yet rootless, like mistletoe; owing nothing to the soil, giving nothing to it and getting nothing of it in return."

As a parting gift, Clell pointed to shelves of mushrooms clinging to the base of oak trunks. Like mistletoe, they leach nutrients from the tree, he said. Mushrooms attached to trunks signal that the tree is struggling to survive. All species in the woods support Darwin's observations that there are variations among members of the same species, but none more so than the mushroom. Within thirty yards, we saw semi-oval mushroom shelves attached to lower oak trunks, tiny white beaded parasols, bright red hats atop curved white stems, and large flat saucers. Several Chicken of the Woods mushrooms had exploded from a fallen trunk—edible fleshy orange and pink disks. Those attached to barks took months to develop, Clell said; others, more lithe and colorful, sprouted from the earth overnight. My favorite mushroom had a compact, curved stem and a red bonnet. Overnight, "discreetly, very quietly," as Sylvia Plath wrote in her poem "Mushrooms," the drooping red cap would be transformed into an open umbrella.

A few days later, I sallied into the woods on my own. After spending time with Jim and Clell, I saw some of the flora more clearly. Even so, an air of mystery lingered in the shadows. I understood how ancient cultures could worship trees, and why sacred groves had been places of religious practice. When Darwin roamed the valley of the Rio Negro in Patagonia, he caught sight of a tree famous among the natives, known as the altar of Walleechu.*

> As soon as a tribe of Indians come in sight of it, they offer their adorations by loud shouts. . . . Poor Indians, not having anything better, only pull a thread out of their ponchos, and fasten it to the tree. Richer Indians are accustomed to pour spirits and maté into a certain hole, and likewise to smoke upwards, thinking thus to afford all possible gratification to Walleechu.

To capture this spiritual feeling, the Japanese invented a practice called forest bathing—the custom of renewing one's mind and body with a walk in the woods. Scientific

*From Darwin's *The Voyage of the Beagle*

evidence supports the value of an old-fashioned pensive meander. With a deep breath, you will inhale oils from conifers that reduce blood pressure, boost the immune system, and decrease the stress hormone cortisol. The negative air ions ease depression and activate hormones: dehydroepiandrosterone, which protects against heart disease, obesity, and diabetes; and adiponectin, which guards against atherosclerosis. The bacteria in the mycelial network boost the immune system, fight depression, and help maintain the microbiome (the bacteria on the skin and in the intestines).

Thoreau saw wildness in his walk in the woods. For him, primitive vigor, animal spirits, and atavistic urges link us to what is fundamentally human and protect us against mind-numbing daily labor and the alienation of corporate conformity. His essay "Walking" ended with crossing a metaphorical border, into the Holy Land, after waking up to nature and shedding "our employments and habits of thought." It is a sort of medical recovery, a crossing into "the health and soundness of Nature." It was a personal resurrection that also had the power to rewrite American history. For the person who celebrates nature's wildness, "where he lives no fugitive slave laws are passed." And for those whose minds and hearts breathed fresh forest air, they shall experience their own "great awakening."

After my walks in the woods, I could not boast of a personal great awakening. Jim taught me about local history and Clell unleashed a steady flow of facts about pines and oaks. I turned toward home after my fourth walk, my plaid shirt laden with sweat, my sleeves laced with gossamer cobwebs, and my mind buttressed with details of dendrology. I walked home slowly and breathed deeply, hoping to inhale some of the miracle chemicals that the leaves had exhaled. As I exited the woods and entered an open pasture, I knew I had left a vast ecosystem of death and decay as well as a land of magic.

Dangers of Meditation

At dawn I stood before a fallen giant, its dozen arms cracked and splayed along the twenty-foot trunk. A thunderous crash at midnight announced the collapse of a cypress tree due west of the house. Now armed for battle, I lowered the visor of my safety helmet, depressed the chainsaw throttle, and gripped the starter-cord handle.

Most of my work in the fields—manicuring woods, mowing pastures, planting buckwheat and clover—requires focus. Chain-sawing demands intense concentration. Injuries to amateurs abound in local stories. One doctor told me of a wife who surprised her husband as he lowered his chainsaw into a pile of firewood. When he turned to protect his rear, his saw jumped backwards and cleaved into his skull. I listened in horror while another doctor regaled me with a tale of a patient who pushed the tip of the saw into bark and watched as the chain recoiled into a leg artery.

I was determined to prevent any similar disaster, so I considered my strategy before pulling the starter cord. The labor required to reduce this Goliath to manageable chunks was daunting—and would eventually turn monotonous and frustrating. I needed to gird my loins. The safest strategy would be to empty my mind of all distractions. Any interruption or daydream could result in disaster. I pictured myself tangled with limb-severing machinery, then took deep breaths and released them slowly, remembering Peri's mindfulness instructions. Whenever she and I lay awake in the middle of the night, she would remind me how to breathe. "One gentle inhale; one long, slow exhale. Repeat." Within minutes she would achieve a deep REM dream state. I remained fidgeting beside her as troubling memories rushed my mental floodgates.

Determined to calm all intruding thoughts, I followed Peri's breathing instructions and yanked the starter cord. My mind seemed empty enough at first, but I soon remembered the last time I tried meditation: I had veered my tractor into a ditch. After severing a few branches, I knew that meditation was going to save neither life nor limb. Distracting thoughts were already jostling each other in my head: Why did I spit into the lowered helmet guard? Did I remember to wash my coffee cup before Peri could find it? Why was a turkey vulture circling?

Worse, boredom, the complimentary evil to distraction, was already creeping in. I might maintain focus during a mundane task, but boredom would crush my spirit. Andy Warhol once claimed, "I like boring things," but for me boredom only made my labor more tedious—and in this case, more dangerous. Adam Smith had warned of the dangers of boredom. It all started with pins. *The Wealth of Nations* began with a discussion of the division of labor in the pin factory he had visited. "One man draws out the wire, another straightens it, a third cuts it, a fourth points it, a fifth grinds it at the top for receiving the head."

Hence the production of pins vastly increased. But a thousand pages later Smith warned about the downside of capitalist progress. The person "whose whole life is spent in performing a few simple operations . . . generally becomes as stupid and ignorant as it is possible for a human creature to become." The boredom generated from the repetition of simple tasks, wrote Smith, rendered people incapable of rational conversation or tender sentiment. Indeed, in the first half hour of chain-sawing, I had turned into Smith's dullard.

I needed a new strategy to calm my pesky thoughts while not descending into mindless boredom. My hands vibrating from the saw, the chain spewing sawdust, I began singing bits of songs and reciting favorite poems. Reciting poetry to oneself in the fields can seem ludicrous, but it refreshed my mind, dulled by dust and sweat. More than two millennia before me, Virgil saw the utility of singing on the farm. In his early poem "Moretum," the rustic husbandman Symilus performed his own seemingly endless task. In tireless circles his right hand turned a mill while the left supplied the grain. To salve the dullness, he sang country ditties as his weary hands toiled. Virgil's nearly forgotten poem came in handy when the Revolutionary generation sought a motto for their new country. For breakfast, Symilus ground herbs, cheese, and garlic with a mortar and pestle to make a sort of pesto. Out of the many colors, wrote Virgil, came one—*e pluribus unum*.

Like the ancient Roman farmer, I sang to counteract a confluence of miseries: the dullness of my labor, the solitude of the daily grind, and the intrusion of painful thoughts. When my back ached from holding my arms outstretched and my legs in a slightly crouched position, and when I waxed nostalgic for the stronger back of my lost youth, Joni Mitchell's "Both Sides Now" wafted through my head. When I found myself mulling over my mortality, Leonard Cohen's "Hallelujah" comforted me. When my mood soared with optimism, I recited Gerard Manley Hopkins's "The Windhover"—and when it sank into depression, his "Carrion Comfort." I fell into a rhythm and chain-sawed for an hour, scarcely aware that I was singing to myself.

Sharing a few moments with Mitchell, Cohen, and Hopkins gave me the illusion of companionship. When the saw sputtered for lack of fuel, however, I was awakened to my solitary state. It is easy to confuse solitude with rugged individualism. There is a certain American pride associated with Daniel Boone or Natty Bumppo, the historical and fictional archetypes of the resourceful wilderness survivor. And Emerson justified the ideal of the pioneer in his "Self-Reliance," which apotheosized non-conformity, reliance on one's instinct, and autonomy. But as I worked the land, I simultaneously held the contradictory notion that I was never truly alone. Before I ever mounted a tractor, I sought advice from local experts and received encouragement from colleagues. I was surrounded by resources, from fuel and seed to tools and straw. However solitary I might feel, every movement I made was informed by a community.

This pendulum swing from radical individualism to community, appeared in the Puritan colonies and continued throughout American philosophy and literature. Emerson's energetic defense of self-reliance was almost immediately rejected by other American thinkers. Melville's Captain Ahab was a dark parody of Emerson, an obsessed hero who embodied the deranged extreme to which a solitary, autonomous actor might travel. Orestes Brownson rejected Emerson's version of transcendentalism from another direction. For Brownson, the community was the important actor. Social arrangements underwrote both self-reliance and conformity and determined good outcomes or evils and obsessions. Radical thinkers sought redress in social change, not (as Thoreau would have it) simply in waking one's neighbors up.

As I sawed that day, I mused that farmers are in many respects the philosophical opposite of the pioneer. They may work alone and feel the daily drudge of it, but they rely on a community. They do not wander or explore, they remain on their plot of land. Of course, they may have trekked across a continent or sailed across an ocean to find that plot—the intersection of pioneer and farmer is the space that Willa Cather inhabits—but in general farmers are not hunter-gatherers, they are part of the agricultural revolution. They cannot flee a community that makes them uncomfortable, for they have made a commitment. Their names rarely enter history books. And as Thomas Hardy noticed in his poem "In Time of 'The Breaking of Nations,'" the steady rhythm of these anonymous tillers of the soil will outlast royal lineages, wars, and other temporary outbursts of history.

I

Only a man harrowing clods
  In a slow silent walk
With an old horse that stumbles and nods
  Half asleep as they stalk.

II

Only thin smoke without flame
  From the heaps of couch-grass;
Yet this will go onward the same
  Though Dynasties pass.

III

Yonder a maid and her wight
  Come whispering by:
War's annals will cloud into night
  Ere their story die.

Sawing the cypress branches occupied most of the morning. Reducing the trunk to dozens of two-foot cylinders took another three days. Like Hardy's field workers, I felt distant from the happenings of the world beyond the farm and riveted to my own plot of land. An anonymous farm hand, I doubted whether I could outlast war's annals, but at least I had conquered the dangers of a motorized chainsaw and punishing thoughts.

Magical Realism

From our house, several pastures extend in every direction. Oliver, the elderly horse, roamed in one rolling field, swatting flies and munching rye. The other fields begged for mowing every fortnight. One drops so steeply from the driveway that my tractor threatens to overturn every time I make the descent. The largest lies behind the barn, its acres a buffer between civilization and the woods.

Grass sprouted quickly after a few June showers. One morning, while scraping oak pollen out of the gutters and spreading mulch in Peri's gardens, I plotted my mowing route through half of the open fields. When, at noon, I started to make my way through the fields, I saw with an analytical mind. The bright glare of sunlight cleansed the woods and pastures. It acted like an antiseptic, stripping nature of all imaginings and metaphors. In the bright glare, I noticed nature waning: insect holes bored into tree trunks, weeds crowding out flowers and herbs, and fallen branches spotted with green fungus.

Toward evening I was on my second tank of gas and growing weary. Despite my flagging energy, there was something about the sky, suspended between day and night, that ignited my imagination. The earth slowly prepared for nightfall, and cardinals and finches, perched on several levels of branches, were shimmering bulbs on a Christmas tree. Trees themselves seemed to move, their dusky outlines hovering over my miniscule human form. It was easy to imagine how archaic Greeks came to believe the oaks of Dodona whispered oracles and why the Druids consulted the Rowan trees for divine guidance.

For me the most significant talking tree was the one cut down to make Jesus's cross in the Old English poem "Dream of the Rood," the earliest dream poem in English. The Anglo-Saxon rood, or cross, told how it suffered nail wounds and spear thrusts and felt sorrow for being the instrument of Christ's crucifixion. Dante encountered talking trees in the infernal realm of the suicides. Transformed into gnarled trees, tormented by harpies who snapped their branches for eternity, the damned who surrendered to despair lament only their own suffering.

My childhood favorite was the cranky apple tree in *The Wizard of Oz,* angry at Dorothy for picking its fruit. Baum's great-grandson Roger wrote a sequel, *Dorothy of Oz,* whose talking trees, which grew on the banks of the Munchkin River, sacrificed their limbs so that Dorothy and her colleagues could make a boat. Tolkien's talking trees in *The Two Towers,* like Great Burnham Wood in *Macbeth,* marched to war to fight a tyrant. The Ents, normally patient and deliberate, became roused with slow-boiling anger when Saruman's armies mowed down many of their neighbors.

At noon all the world had seemed still. Everything was in motion now at dusk. It was at a similar liminal moment that Darwin, near the forests of Rio de Janeiro, commented that succulent plants assumed "most fantastical forms." For me, now that the sun had descended just below the horizon, the russet rays refracted in the atmosphere and the air shimmered. Small branches in the grass became snakes, six-winged dragonflies became fairies, and the cacophony of frogs and cicadas hinted of mysterious, invisible forces.

I think it is no wonder that Romantic poets from Wordsworth to Stevens divided the world between the sun and the moon—the sun representing the analytical, objective mind that sees the world as it is, the moon representing the imaginative ways the mind imposes itself upon the world. For Emily Dickinson, the mind could create magic even without the world:

> To make a prairie it takes a clover and one bee,
> One clover, and a bee.
> And revery.
> The revery alone will do,
> If bees are few.

Dickinson didn't need the bee for her revery, but Thoreau turned the bee into a figure for his imagination. His thoughts originated in the mundane world, but his senses were alive enough not to get mired there. A passage in his *Journal* captured how his mind wandered like a bee in the fields.

> The scenery, when it is truly seen, reacts on the life of the seer. How to live. How to get the most life. How to extract its honey from the flower of the world. That is my every-day business. I am as busy as a bee about it. I ramble over all fields on that errand, and am never so happy as when I feel myself heavy with honey and wax. I am like a bee

> searching the livelong day for the sweets of nature. Do I not impregnate and intermix the flowers, produce rare and finer varieties by transferring my eyes from one to another?

I had more work to do that day than extracting honey from the flower of the world. My errand was keeping nature's growth at bay. When I dismounted my mower that evening, my arms shaking from the machine's vibration, I felt a tired happiness for my day's labor. Then grumbling apple trees and angry Ents filled my head as I walked toward the house.

Nocturnal Adventures

After a morning of chores and a long afternoon mowing in the sun, my limbs were sluggish. In the evening I moved in slow motion toward the couch and collapsed feeling at once drowsy and restless. Gradually losing consciousness, I thought sleep would come swiftly. But despite my languor, the quiet stillness of the world lured me outdoors.

As usual, my slightest movement activated my Doberman, who lurched upwards and trotted to the porch door. In the yard, all was silent; all human and animal activity had ceased. The darkness and quiet swaddled me as I walked past Peri's garden into the fields. Though set, the sun still dully brightened the night sky. Soon, however, it drew its rays inward. The moon was new, so the flowers and trees were veiled in darkness. The only beauty now was in the stars. And in a sense of solitude. "If a man would be alone," Emerson wrote in *Nature*, "let him look at the stars."

Unlike me, ancient farmers did not write about shimmering beauty in the stars as much as they read advice about their crops. Constellations marked their seasonal tasks. "When the Pleiades, daughters of Atlas, are rising," Hesiod explained in *Works and Days*,

> begin your harvest, and your ploughing when they are going to set. . . . Winnow Demeter's holy grain,

> when strong Orion first appears, on a smooth threshing-floor in an airy place. . . . But when Orion and Sirius are come into mid-heaven, and rosy-fingered Dawn sees Arcturus, then cut off all the grape-clusters.

Modern almanacs support Archaic Greek astronomical wisdom. They advise that Earth signs (Taurus, Virgo, and Capricorn) are good for planting root crops, and that it's a good time to cultivate soil and harvest during Air signs (Gemini, Libra, and Aquarius).

I was skeptical. I found myself agreeing with Ben Franklin, ever the scientist and cultural observer, who poked fun at the wisdom of the stars and looked through the other end of the telescope. "Whatever may be the Musick of the Spheres," he wrote in his *Poor Richard's Almanac*, "how great soever the Harmony of the Stars, 'tis certain there is no Harmony among the Stargazers." Wendell Berry took the traditional view. In his poem "The Contrariness of the Mad Farmer," he proudly announced that he had "planted by the stars in defiance of the experts, / and tilled somewhat by incantation and by singing, / and reaped, as I knew, by luck and Heaven's favor, / in spite of the best advice."

Approaching the woods, I proceeded with extreme caution, looking upward only briefly, lest I stumble into a nocturnal copperhead or skunk. The night sky blanketed the hemisphere, but dense foliage hid the stars just above the horizon. I could see constellations only by craning my neck for a view past the towering oaks and pines. Walking east down one path, Orion strode overhead, his belt pointing south toward Sirius, the dog star. Turning around, I spied Ursa major, the big dipper's handle pointing to Polaris in Ursa minor. Whenever I got turned around in the dark (easy to do while trying to reign in a Doberman sniffing a frog), the constellations settled me.

The transition from a darkening sky to pitch black came suddenly. The instant it did, I was alert to the nocturnal sounds of the wild. The rhythmic chirping of katydids burst into the darkness as loud as a tractor engine. The choral croaking of frogs reminded me of the mathematical precision of Baroque counterpoint. Now and then a coyote howled, piercing the monotonous and deafening music, signaling to her partner that prey was near, and warning me to keep the dog by my side.

Nightfall reminded me of episodes in *Fantasia* when hibernating creatures awakened and romped. I sidestepped frogs the size of almonds; those the size of grapefruits squatted just as oblivious. Some leaped at the speed of slingshots; others were as heavy as Twain's frog of Calaveras County. I read that a frog shortage has plagued every state in the Union, except for North Carolina. It wasn't always so. Loren Eiseley heard of a friend's encounter with a multitude of frogs at nightfall in "The Dance of the Frogs" chapter in *The Star Thrower*. "Thousands of them, and twenty species, trilling, gurgling, and grunting in as many keys."

A neighbor passed by Thoreau one morning, who was standing with his hands behind him, staring ahead of him, and found him in the same position when he returned that evening. "He kept on lookin' down at that pond, and he said, as if he was thinkin' about the stars in the heavens, 'Mr. Murray, I'm a-studyin'—the habits—of the bullfrog!"

At Hyacinth Farm, hundreds of frogs roam the property at night, emerging from their holes or leaping from the creek. The dogs give chase, noses to the ground, but seem confused about what to do when they get close. It is difficult to tell in the dark whether our population consists of green frogs, Southern leopard frogs, Carolina gopher frogs, or wood frogs. I am happy to host them, regardless of species, crisscrossing the grounds, as they eat insects and spiders. I presume snakes and owls eat them in turn.

The cacophony of frogs reached an ear-piercing pitch when myriad croaks let loose in tandem. The monotonous croaking canceled out all other sense impressions. So deafening are frogs that they gave the goddess Athena a royal headache, and her annoyance inspired her to reject Zeus's request to help them in "The Battle of the Frogs and Mice." "I will not help them," complained the mock-epic Athena, "for they also are not considerate: once, when I was returning early from war, I was very tired, and though I wanted to sleep, they would not let me even doze a little for their outcry; and so I lay sleepless with a headache until cock-crow."

Thoreau captured a similar moment in his *Journal*:

> It was shortly after dusk, thousands of frogs were croaking in a deafening roar. A low mist hung above the water. In that direction, the sparkle of the planet Venus was multiplied by countless ripples, the light from each reflection haloed by the

> mist. Meanwhile, above the adjacent meadows, the coppery light of fireflies was multiplying as dusk gave way to dark. This was a river summer scene that no forest or field could match.

Thoreau returned a few times in his *Journal* to nocturnal encounters with frogs. He painted humorous scenes as he stared at wide-eyed frogs, who patiently stared back. He also noticed how inert frogs seemed, as if they assumed that humans were not natural predators. I have often been teased with the thought experiment of the frog in the pot of water, refusing to jump out as the water is slowly heated to the boiling point. How ridiculous, from the point of natural selection, to think that a creature would not reach a point of discomfort before succumbing to extinction. But frogs, like many humans, do indeed resist reacting to threatening stimuli. Only this morning, astride my riding mower, I persisted as drops of sweat became torrents burning my eyes, and as an allergic sniffle expanded into dozens of successive sneezes.

I watched in amazement as my dog's nose, sweeping the ground, arrived at a frog that could not seem to summon the energy to leap out of danger. When I tried to intervene, boots gently shoving the frog out of the dog's path, the creature did not budge. Perhaps it was this frog I later observed wriggling in the beak of a chicken haughtily dashing away from its colleagues toward a private feast.

*I Tell You, War Is Hell**

The June morning was muggy, and the earth smelled of rain. I spent the dawn hours digging holes and planting bushes for Peri's garden. My shoulders recoiled after every thrust of the shovel into the stubborn russet clay. Steadily colliding with rocks and roots, the steel blade of my spade cracked. Weary and sweat-soaked, I felt as disjointed as my shovel. As the clouds darkened and it started to drizzle, I headed for the woods to give my muscles a few moments to recover.

The respite was shattered when my boot snagged a thorny smilax vine, which clamped to the earth at one-yard intervals in its crawl toward a pine trunk. Sprawled at ground level, I faced what would become my mortal enemy, Japanese stiltgrass. I remained on my knees for the next forty-five minutes, uprooting bunches of the stuff and tossing them into piles. Subconsciously I knew this was wasted energy. I was scattering seeds that would sprout the following spring. I could not eradicate acres of this invader. Still, I persisted.

The sky darkened further, but the canopy prevented a barrage of raindrops from reaching me. Moments of satisfaction poked through my weed-pulling haze as when I tore enough of the stiltgrass to reveal the base of a giant

*From William Tecumseh Sherman's 1879 speech to the graduating class of the Michigan Military Academy

oak, its massive roots creeping into the earth. But that feeling swiftly yielded to frustration. The grass extended in every direction and onto the base of nearby oaks and pines. My weeding seemed endless and futile, like trying to stop ocean waves from smashing into the sand. It was also mentally debilitating, wrenching my attention from a more pleasant stream of consciousness or from one of the more valuable tasks that might have punctuated the day. The grass was a black hole, pulling me away from my wandering and my work.

The language of war has invaded many worlds. Wherever there are opposing parties, martial metaphors triumph. Viruses invade and white blood cells attack. Quarterbacks throw bullets and bombs, and the defensive line engages in a blitz attack (or is in retreat). Hedge funds raid corporations, new ventures conquer markets, stock prices are pushed into negative territory, investors are on the run, and we face the threat of global financial Armageddon.

My life on the farm is plagued by yet another form of warfare, the enemy of invasive species from distant lands. They often arrive via human transport and take over fields and pastures at an ineluctable pace. These worthy opponents have no will to power and no thought of aggression, just the urge to survive. They take over with no natural opposition, more like Sherman's march through the deep South to the sea than his army battling Joe Johnston's. In fact, they resemble colonizers more than armies. They cross oceans, like Hernando de Soto or Hernán Cortés, put down roots, spread quickly, take resources away from natives, and prove intractable.

Many plant invaders came to the Americas from

Asia: stiltgrass, wisteria, hydrilla, and the tree of heaven all originated in China or Japan. Some of these had innocent and even useful functions. Japanese stiltgrass was used as a packing material. Kudzu was imported in the nineteenth century for erosion control and livestock forage. The tree of heaven was ornamental. The sea road from Asia to America was paved with good intentions, but all of these plants ended up being as helpful as umbrellas in the Mojave.

When I arrived at Hyacinth Farm, I discovered trees of heaven with trunk diameters over ten inches rooted next to the barn. That girth (and corresponding height) required several hours of chain-sawing. Unfortunately, I'm not equipped to extract the medicinal properties of the leaves, which Chinese medical texts claim can treat a wide range of ailments, including mental illness and baldness. And although the tree is a host plant for silkworms native to China, local bees, butterflies, and birds avoid it. It crowds out native plants and, worse, produces biochemicals that act as natural herbicides, hindering the growth of competing trees.

The tree of heaven is a wily enemy, but my most intense rage is reserved for Japanese stiltgrass. That invasion came suddenly. My forest floors were leaf-covered one year and carpeted with stiltgrass the next. At first, I was charmed. The ankle-high plants had a pillowy texture, with elegant leaves reminiscent of bamboo shoots in Japanese prints. But within weeks the stalks shot two feet upward, rendering the woods impassable.

Removing it would take a significant amount of time, hours I would have to subtract from cleaning the barn, collecting eggs, mowing and tilling, and collecting fallen branches. There are never enough work hours in the day, and hard deadlines come with dusk. Also, "removing" is a euphemism. The roots are shallow, and it is easy to spend hours gently ripping handfuls out of the earth. But the task is as endless as it is fruitless. The remaining plants cast thousands of seeds, which can remain viable for over five years. Every gardener and forester with whom I have commiserated has lamented that it would take many successive years of chemical eradication or controlled burns to banish it from the landscape. Oliver and the chickens avoid it, chiggers and ticks lie in wait on it, and it has no value in the ecosystem. As I emerged from the woods and spread my arms into the steady rain of the open pasture that day that began with digging holes for Peri's garden, the real force of the war metaphor gobsmacked me—I surrendered.

Survival Instinct

Peri and I fell in love with our home at first sight. Its mahogany, oak, redwood, and pine walls radiated warmth and beauty. We failed to take full measure, however, of the woods. All of the pastures were nestled by broad swathes of trees, and acres of dense woods lay behind the barn. Once we unpacked most of the moving boxes, we decided to explore.

We wended our way around fallen limbs and ravines. The air gradually darkened as the canopy choked rays of sunlight. There were no clear paths; and tangled branches and vines loomed in every direction. For a moment, there was something awe-inspiring in nature untouched by human meddling. But there was a subtler, invisible force that infiltrated my consciousness and caused my heart to thump. Simply put, there was a messiness in nature, the tangle of pathless vegetation that rendered me unable to align my mental compass. The sublime and quiet loveliness turned ugly when I realized we were lost. Then other anxieties flooded my mind in our new rural landscape. The heavily wooded slopes offered holes for the unwary in which to snap an ankle. Trees hosted ticks and vines of poison ivy to challenge immune systems. Snakes, quietly nesting amidst leaves and rocks, angered when surprised.

At first, we had reveled in feeling disoriented. Being lost in the woods was, after all, temporary solace from the rigid structures of urban life. But the deep woods ultimately injected us with a sense of primal threat. Peri and I responded differently to being lost in the woods. I wanted to forge ahead until we reached a clearing or another house. We would have to move randomly; navigating by the sun was useless, as it was in its late afternoon descent. Peri, a modern woman impatient with male pioneers, asked directions—she opened the map app on her phone. The signal was weak and intermittent, but it pointed us toward a road. Twenty minutes later the woods delivered us to a street that connected our house to town. We had zig-zagged a few miles through the woods but hewed closely to the road to find our way back.

I emerged from the woods with a rage for order. I had butted against chaotic tree patterns, creeks that meandered across property boundaries, and vines that impeded progress. I needed a strategy to gain control, or at least the illusion of control, amidst the chaos of nature. Any strategy is by definition artificial, a word that once signaled high praise (before the Romantic era demoted it to the mechanical and industrial hell of the modern world). In my first couple of years, I have employed a few traditional strategies. First, there was the Capability Brown strategy: I have weeded, trimmed, chain-sawed, and hacked the land, making it look as if pastures flowed naturally into woods and woods into creeks. I have carved paths through the woods, making them appear less impenetrable. I have laid out gardens, in which Peri arranged plants by size or color. Building stone borders gave the illusion of control over nature.

And then there was the Wallace Stevens strategy of

placing an object in nature to organize the landscape, as he does in his lyric "Anecdote of the Jar."

> I placed a jar in Tennessee,
> And round it was, upon a hill.
> It made the slovenly wilderness
> Surround that hill.
>
> The wilderness rose up to it,
> And sprawled around, no longer wild.
> The jar was round upon the ground
> And tall and of a port in air.
>
> It took dominion everywhere.
> The jar was gray and bare.
> It did not give of bird or bush,
> Like nothing else in Tennessee.

It worked out nicely for me that Stevens placed his jar in a Southern state—perhaps nature in his native North was too heavily overlaid with street grids, housing developments, and factories. Tennessee represented overgrown nature, the sprawling wilderness not yet organized by human hands. The simple jar focused the mind, which calmed the unframed wildness of nature. It also made a philosophical point: we don't really see nature until something human intervenes.

I placed a cast iron monstrosity, an antique cotton-candy machine, in an untended part of the open woods behind the house. A short, stout three-legged cylinder topped with a turquoise basin, this strange creature centered my field of vision. It also invited a certain kind of meditation. Staring at such a contraption reminded me of recent generations of humble farm workers, and how the mechanical intruded upon nature.

In the woods more distant from the house, there was a man-made natural object that evoked a different kind of historical consciousness. Surrounded by pines and oaks, earthworks stretching for dozens of yards were the remains of Confederate redoubts and trenches (not far from Sherman's path as he rode from Richmond to Hillsborough and then on to Durham, where Johnston surrendered almost 90,000 troops from North Carolina, South Carolina, Georgia, and Florida). They helped keep me focused on the fact that I am an intruder in this Southern dust, and that I can scarcely enter the consciousness of the Americans who lost the war and the local farmers who suffered such devastation.

So, nineteenth-century mounds have reshaped one corner of the landscape and an early twentieth-century machine helped organize another. What I found next was twenty-first-century works of art, metal sculptures that could be bolted deeply into the clay. I placed one full of vertical, whimsical energy in the midst of our circular thyme garden. A second sculpture, a combination of a large chained rim, a chemical canister, and a large plate, reassembled to evoke a Buddhist monastery bell, announced the house to visitors swerving up the driveway. I set a third Zen-like meditative piece before a lush arrangement of trees and bushes.

Each sculpture combined jarring pairs of qualities: the dense and the seemingly weightless; classical line and baroque curve; the serious and the playful; the geometric and the Eastern contemplative; grace and sturdiness. They are monuments to the ability of the human mind to hold incompatible ideas in solution.

The Confederate mound, the simple machine, the metal sculptures—a wide spectrum of material, purpose, expertise, and creativity. Each human-made artifact invited me to see order amidst a formless natural expanse. Each piece has continued to lock in my gaze as it organizes the landscape around it. Thus, they create something out of nothing, meaning out of formlessness.

This American oxymoron brought to mind the apparently simple last line of the Stevens poem. "In Tennessee" echoed the first line, thus making the poem as circular, and artificial, as the jar. The poem is a brief meditation on the artificial and how it offers meaning. The first part of the line, "like nothing else," sounds innocent, unartistic, and folksy. There is no doubt about its meaning—it is slang for "unique." But the phrase is also a simile, a strange one that compares something to nothing. Rather, something comes from nothing. Nature for Stevens was formless; order and meaning came from human artifacts placed in a silent landscape.

I Did My Best, It Wasn't Much

A host of brittle azalea limbs attacked me as I tried to wield my branch cutter. Half a dozen bushes, planted in front of the house three decades ago, had sprouted haphazardly for years. Unpruned, some branches stretched high enough to peek over the roof. Others meshed with neighboring bushes, creating a wall of stiff, entangled limbs. Neighbors across the road told me these bushes were the pride of the town. Every April a string of cars would cruise up the driveway, packed with visitors who marveled at the vibrant pinks and sparkling whites.

Because the azaleas had survived beyond their expected lifespan, Peri had launched into active palliative care, sending me on a mission to prune. I was able to snap dozens of dead branches by hand, but a few limbs had grown so thick that only a branch trimmer could hack through them. Ensnarled in one of the bushes, with shorter branches poking my arms and neck, I disturbed a few bumblebees. With my range of motion limited to a few inches, I prayed the bees would soon find pistils and stamens in nearby blossoms.

My interest in bees began in early childhood when my grandmother told me a fairy tale about a mother and her three daughters. She learned the tale from her mother in a Cretan mountain village in the early years of the last century. The story explained why honey was blessed while reinforcing the virtue of filial piety:

> Once upon a time there was a poor mother with four children—three daughters and a son. She was a good mother and raised her children to be virtuous. They all got married and lived happily with their families. The mother was now living on her own. One day she fell ill and needed help. She asked a neighbor to fetch her son to help her. The son was outside fixing his fence and planting bushes. The neighbor said to the son that his mother was sick and needed him. "Don't you see I am busy," the son replied angrily. "I cannot go now." The neighbor returned and told the mother that her son was too busy to help her. The mother cursed her son. "I wish all those bushes would grow on his back." And the son became the porcupine.
>
> "Now please go and ask my eldest daughter to come," said the mother. When the neighbor went to fetch her, she was weaving, making material for clothes. "Please come to help your mother, who is sick," said the neighbor. "I am very busy—can't you see I am weaving? I have to finish, and I cannot leave." The neighbor returned to the mother with this excuse, and the mother cursed her child. "Let her continue to weave. May she never be finished, and may people destroy whatever she makes." And the eldest daughter became the spider.
>
> "Now go tell my second daughter to come." When the neighbor came upon the daughter she was bent over a washtub, scrubbing clothes. "Your

mother needs you, please come with me to her home." "I cannot," said the daughter, "I have to do the wash." The neighbor returned to the mother for the third time with the daughter's excuse. "May she carry the washtub on her back for all time," said the mother. And the daughter became the turtle.

"Please ask my youngest daughter to come," pleaded the mother. And the neighbor went to the mother's last child. She was making bread in the kitchen. Her hands and face were white with flour, for she was kneading dough. But as soon as she heard that her mother was sick, she put down the flour and the dough, washed her hands, and ran to her mother's house. "What can I do for you, mother," she asked? "I will do anything for you."

Her mother was so pleased that she blessed her youngest daughter. "May you be helpful to everybody and may everybody love you." And she became the honeybee, and flew from the window and started making honey, and wax for candles.*

Sadly, I rarely observed bees hovering around our flowers and bushes. The American bumblebee has declined in number by about 90% in recent years. The rusty patched bumblebee and Hawaiian yellow-faced bee have been placed on the endangered species list. As I stood in the midst of the azalea blossoms, I decided to

*My grandmother told me this fairy tale many times during my childhood. I transcribed this and several other tales in my book on Crete, *Dandelions and Honey: Notes on a Forsaken Island.*

do my small part in addressing the bee crisis by planting a pollinator-friendly crop. A few days later I visited a local beekeeper, who suggested buckwheat. I purchased a 50-pound bag of seeds and researched how to prepare the field for planting. The County Soil and Water experts told me that given my land coordinates, my soil was Georgeville silt loam, which was perfect for buckwheat and has been known to yield 55 bushels of rye per acre and 94 bushels of oats.

My tractor has slightly more horsepower than a horse, achieving maximum speed of five miles per hour (on a downslope). I can drag a tiller or a plough behind me but must constantly raise any implement over roots and rocks. Because buckwheat seeds need to be planted only a fraction of an inch below the surface—landing in furrows is supposed to anchor them enough to begin sending down roots—a friend welded a tool for me to scratch the surface and slightly upturn the soil. It looked like a row of blackened front teeth in the broad mouth of an ogre with a symmetrical smile.

The next morning, I hefted the tilling tool onto the tractor hitch. I dragged the metal teeth, careful to lightly scrape the ground. I had been warned that tilling, a more radical intervention, would destroy the microbiome, the ecological community in the soil of microorganisms. Bacteria, archaea, protists, fungi, and viruses are crucial for our immune systems, enzyme production, and plant nutrients, among other things. When the scraping was finished, I planted buckwheat seeds with a walk-behind seeder. A seed drill or a mechanical seeder were beyond my expertise to manage. I fed the seeds into a small spreader and walked boustrophedon—an appropriate word for my level of farming skill, meaning as the ox plows.

Tumultuous rainstorms followed over two successive days, washing away the seeds and flattening the furrows. I blamed the weather rather than my farming methods for the lack of a rich crop that spring. As the prophet Haggai said, "you have sown so much but harvested so little." Fortunately, bees can fly a mile or two in pursuit of pollen before returning to the hive, and we have woods full of tree blossoms. The bees might produce honey despite my abortive attempt at planting. Apparently, reading Cato's farming advice in his *De Re Rustica* (following in Thoreau's footsteps) was not sufficient these days, and I will have to wait until the fall, when I'm told I could try to plant crimson clover for the pollinators.

My farming method lies between the ancient and the modern. The ancient method, which in my area of North Carolina continued up to the mid-twentieth century, comprised a single farmer, a horse or mule-drawn plough, and no fertilizer. Pictures of local farmers in the 1930s resemble Walker Evans's portraits of weary folk in overalls in *Let Us Now Praise Famous Men.* County and municipal governments intervened, attempting to upgrade farming methods to reduce labor and increase yield. Van Woodward labeled this transformation the Bulldozer Revolution.

> The roar and groan and dust of it greet one on the outskirts of every Southern city. . . . The great machine with the lowered blade symbolizes the

> revolution in several respects: in its favorite area of operation, the area where city meets country; in its relentless speed; in its supreme disregard for obstacles, its heedless methods; in what it demolishes and in what it builds.

When I taught the *Gospels* in a world literature course, I did not focus enough on the plight of ancient Palestinian farmers, fishermen, laborers, tax collectors, shepherds, stewards, soldiers, and beggars. Instead, I tried to tease allegorical meaning out of terse verses. The stuff of the parables, coins and seeds and so on, were scaffolding, to be deconstructed once we arrived at theological truth. But life on the farm had the virtue of putting biblical parables into a realistic perspective. Once I moved, it soon became obvious that these anecdotes spoke brutal truths to contemporaries trying to earn a living in difficult circumstances.

The sower in Luke's parable lived by what he grew. It was not only a salvation allegory when his seeds fell by the wayside, were devoured by fowl, fell upon rock, landed on thorns, or fell on fertile soil. It was a matter of survival. In its compression, and in its allegorical drive, the parable also left out other reasons for a farmer's failure. In my case the seeds did not fall on rocks. I was too inexperienced to till and plant successfully. Or I may have simply had bad luck, with heavy rains washing away soil and seed.

A sermon on a recent Sunday reminded me of the ancient holiday of Rogation Day. It sounded like an opportunity to pray for hair. Rather, it is a holy day to pray for agricultural health. There are technically several Rogation Days, and the so-called minor ones are on the liturgical calendar preceding Ascension (forty days after Easter). Minor Rogation days were first celebrated in the late fifth century by Mamertus, Bishop of Vienne in France. The faithful fasted in preparation for Ascension and prayed for relief from natural disasters. In the case of early medieval Vienne, just south of Lyon on the Rhone, the disasters included wheat rust, wolves, earthquakes, and drought.

Mamertus led his parishioners to the boundaries of the parish, where the community prayed in unison. I sympathized with the devoted who relied upon this mode of prayer. Asking for a gift in return for one's faith and weekly church attendance is all too human. But I preferred a different mode in which the stricken Job debated with God, questioned unjust suffering, and dared God to answer. In either case, praying at the boundaries, a ceremony called beating the bounds, was the least subtle Christian appropriation of pagan liturgical practice, in this case, a Roman festival in which revelers walked to a grove several miles from the city to perform fertility rites (which in turn sounded similar to the Eleusinian procession from Athens to the outskirts to perform cult rituals). The Christian calendar overlapped with pagan festivals, and fertility cycles underlay both. Unfortunately, I had neglected to perform any rite before sowing my seed.

Weeks and months after I sowed buckwheat and crimson clover seeds, only weeds sprouted. My bees had to fend for themselves in distant pastures. If I had been an ancient farmer, I might have been concerned with my salvation. More urgently, my family would have starved. As Leonard Cohen lamented, "I did my best. It wasn't much."*

*From Leonard Cohen's song "Hallelujah"

*Nature's First Green Is Gold**

To mark our first anniversary on Hyacinth Farm, Peri and I strolled at twilight through the pastures surrounding our house. The late summer evening's stillness scattered the sun's rays from below the horizon, painting the air around the trees a soft salmon pink. Passing several mounds of fallen branches I had collected over the year, we were alert to nocturnal snakes and woodchuck burrows. Both quiet, we absorbed the beauty of the darkening sky. When we realized that pitch black was only moments away, we turned back toward the house.

Practical details pestered me as I mused over the chores on my ever-expanding list: stones to buy to enclose Peri's terraced gardens; forms to complete to adopt a rescue dog (more rigorous than the procedure to adopt a baby); seeds to select for ground cover; weeds to whack in corners not available to the mower. But these thoughts receded as my mind arranged colors that marked our first annual cycle. The darker the sky grew, the more vivid the colors my imagination painted.

The red bud tree bursts forth first with fuchsia—in February, if the sun warms the earth early enough. Next come the azaleas, with a rich salmony pink and cream. In late winter and early spring, the ground pushes up fifty shades of green: pine, sea, olive, hunter, emerald, sham-

*Title of a Robert Frost poem

rock, Islamic. The color of some curiously shaped weeds reminds me of what stately, plump Buck Mulligan in the "Telemachus" chapter of *Ulysses* labeled "snotgreen"—a color he bequeathed to modern Irish poets and that he playfully claimed derived from the Homeric formula, "the snotgreen sea." Each succeeding spring blesses our pastures with new species of weed, each of which grows at a different pace and becomes increasingly mower-resistant. Erupting in patches of grass, they host shades of green in minor keys—artichoke, sage, pea, chartreuse.

White and orange lilies burst mid-summer, later than the surrounding flowers. Some azalea bushes blossom again in the autumn, joining chrysanthemums (golden, purplish, and rust). Then come the yellows, purples (not as rare in nature as Alice Walker claimed), and deep antique reds of majestic Japanese maples. A dozen of these shimmer in the fall, the loftiest of which rises higher than a two-story house. Local tree specialists call it a "champion," the term they bestow upon the largest specimen of the species. In late autumn the tree fertilizes itself with a vast carpet of fallen vermillion leaves two feet deep.

So, labor is mixed with visual joy. It is the same joy Thoreau felt as he described the red maple and the purple grasses in "Autumnal Tints." His essay is an American epic catalogue of colors and an ode to the power of observation. "When you come to observe faithfully the changes of each humblest plant," he concluded the essay, "you find that each has, sooner or later, its peculiar autumnal tint; and if you undertake to make a complete list of the bright tints, it will be nearly as long as a catalogue of the plants in your vicinity."

Whitman added a melancholy hue to his epic catalogue of plants, what he called his "tallying chant," in "When Lilacs Last in the Dooryard Bloom'd." The poem is a pastoral elegy in the tradition of Milton's "Lycidas" and Shelley's "Adonais." It undulates toward epic, where the catalogue was born. Lilacs, Whitman observed, come first, then roses and lilies, in the annual cycle now plagued by death. The tall lilac bush, "with heart-shaped leaves of rich green," signaled the eternal return of spring as well as the helplessness the poet felt before victorious death.

Whitman's spectrum included the colors Lincoln's funeral train passed as it journeyed westwards—yellow-spear'd wheat, apple-tree blows of white and pink, the pale green leaves of prolific trees. As Lincoln's funeral procession continued, Whitman returned to his observations of heart-shaped leaves of rich green and delicately colored blossoms, as if he sought order and psychological refuge in nature's flowers, leaves, and colors. But he could not escape the oppressive feeling of grief. Like the thrush, he sang a "song of the bleeding throat," alone.*

As I walked in silence, my mind oscillated between Whitman's melancholy and Thoreau's ebullience. I wallowed in the petty miseries of poisonous insect bites, broken machinery, and sprained backs. At times I was paralyzed by memories of failed projects and forebodings of mortality. But this evening was steeped in joy. It was the kind of joy Annie Dillard, using snippets from Van Gogh's letters, expressed in her poem "I Am Trying to Get at Something Utterly Heartbroken": "A ploughed field with clods of violet earth; / Over all a yellow sky

*Walt Whitman's "When Lilacs Last in the Dooryard Bloom'd"

with a yellow sun. / So there is every moment something that moves one intensely."

As we headed homeward, Peri and I shared different memories of colors that had erupted during the year. We had that in common with Thoreau and Whitman—comfort in a world organized by hue. "Hand in hand, with wandering steps and slow," we made our way through our new Eden.*

*From Milton's *Paradise Lost*

Leisure

I awoke before dawn and sensed a stillness in the air. Two thoughts wrestled with one another. I wondered at the glory of the landscape, even in leafless January. Sloping pastures and trees shining with frost filled me with exuberant energy. At the same time, I counted the chores that would choke the morning—trimming bushes, chain-sawing fallen branches, heaving boulders away from the tractor's path.

I yearned for a few hours of quiet—the sort of quiet that miniscule figures in paintings of Thomas Cole or Frederick Church experience amidst sublime landscapes. The main difference between the picturesque view of nature and the farmer's view, however, is leisure. The cultural meaning of leisure has taken a precipitous fall over the millennia. The Greek word for leisure became the English word for school. Leisure was highly valued, not the least because it was necessary for the underpinnings of democratic society, namely, the assembly and the courts. The Latin word *otium* was similarly valued; its opposite, which became the English *negotiate*, signified the less dignified world of business. The concept of leisure somersaulted over the centuries, from a Greek and Roman philosophical virtue to the harsh, negative valence bestowed by the Puritans, for whom it signified the deadly sin of sloth, a selfish disregard for the community, and damnation.

For Aristotle, leisure underwrote democracy, drama, philosophy, mathematics, and every activity that thrived in the city state, a connection he develops in the *Metaphysics* and *Politics*, as well as in the *Nicomachean Ethics*. The modern philosopher who revived Aristotle's notion of leisure, Josef Pieper,* contrasted leisure not only with work but also with idleness. Leisure in this sense allows for contemplation unburdened by economic stress or utility. It is the giving up of the will in order to achieve inner calm, spiritual nourishment, and a noble solitude that is the opposite of loneliness.

So I awakened that January morning to the unresolvable tension of my Greek and Puritan cultural inheritance. Like Wittgenstein's drawing of the rabbit-duck, the landscape keeps shifting into mutually exclusive frames. It signifies work, then radiates wonder and invites meditation. Thoreau's maxim about the power of the mind to create nature ("the landscape radiated from me") was meant to convey his mind's joyful power to create a home wherever he opened his eyes. But it also meant that the view depended upon cultural predispositions. My Puritan identity sees rocks to be moved, logs to be sawed, and pastures to be tilled. My Greek self, which values leisure, sees the potential for a meditative stroll, and sees the world in an iris blossom.

This double strand is part of the American DNA. It appears in various moments of *Walden*. On the one hand, Thoreau was content reading Homer, and he praised William Gilpin, the creator of the picturesque landscape. On the other hand, he was careful to account

*Josef Pieper, *Leisure, the Basis of Culture*

for his tools and seeds, and he valued hoeing his bean field. But the magical fusion of imaginative leisure and hard work was not what he preached. Work for him was part of the meditative process. True hard work, such as the drudgery of the Irish farmer, the Canadian woodchopper, and the railroad workers, was dull and meaningless, in Thoreau's view. He assumed it did not allow for introspection or the appreciation of nature's beauty. In his dismissal of all that Ben Franklin represented in American culture (accounting, hard work, habit, Puritan moral values, philanthropy) he, like Melville, was an early and prescient critic of capitalism and the way work could crush the spirit. But his romantic enthusiasm ran the risk of devaluing labor. It blinded him to the sacrifices farmers made to support their families. And it rendered him incapable of envisioning how communities, as opposed to individuals who can afford to live in the woods, created social networks and infrastructures.

For me the ambiguity of leisure, and therefore also of work, is best captured in the famous last line of James Wright's "Lying in a Hammock at William Duffy's Farm in Pine Island, Minnesota." The title gets details of place, position, and furniture out of the way, making room for a series of wonderful imagistic bursts:

> Over my head, I see the bronze butterfly,
> Asleep on the black trunk,
> Blowing like a leaf in green shadow.
> Down the ravine behind the empty house,
> The cowbells follow one another
> Into the distances of the afternoon.
> To my right,

In a field of sunlight between two pines,
The droppings of last year's horses
Blaze up into golden stones.
I lean back, as the evening darkens and comes on.
A chicken hawk floats over, looking for home.
I have wasted my life.

It is a lazy dusk. The vastly disparate images are related only by the direction the poet casts his gaze: above, below, rightward. There is a hint of helplessness, since there is almost no human agency as the images proceed—the poet sees, of course, but it is the cowbells that follow and the horse droppings that blaze. Then the final thud of moral awakening. This creator of stunning images claims he has wasted his life. He creates images, but that is not enough. By the end of his thirteen lines (an abortive sonnet) he has barely moved. Is there another poem with less motion than leaning back? Even the hawk is in the midst of a journey, an archetypal *nostos* or homecoming. Nor has he even bothered to interpret, or give meaning to, any of the images. In the case of the poet who whiles away the afternoon on a hammock, leisure yields stunning images but nothing yet of significance.

The narrator has nurtured the wrong dreams. Relaxing in William Duffy's hammock, he feels alienated from the kind of work to which he has dedicated his life. He has not performed any meaningful work or engaged in any productive leisure. Observing the natural world in every direction, he sees that the work of the butterfly, the cows, and the hawk are not in conflict with their true nature. He also sees the beauty of their movement and color. Lying prone on the hammock, he begins the work of self-reflection. It is productive leisure. Deciding to engage in meaningful work (he is on a farm, after all) or write a poem would be the next stage of his redemption.

I dressed warmly for the day's labor that winter morning. A Greek coffee brewing on the stove filled the kitchen with a caressing aroma. After several minutes, the haze of sleep evaporated. I braced myself for my chores and thought that the only significance in the morning's drudgery would be crossing a task off my list, attended by a feeling of happy exhaustion. And hands chilled to the bone.

Chickens
and
Other Beasts

I've Got You Under My Skin

Joe was clad in short sleeves, short pants, and sneakers without socks, unfazed by July's glaring sun and brutal heat. An unprepared Yankee, I lumbered behind him with dungarees clinging to my drenched thighs. The former owner of our home had offered to give me a tour of the land when I flew down from New York for the home inspection. Now we were trudging along the path he had carved out with a tractor around the property's boundaries so that he and his wife could stroll through the woods.

I was surprised to learn that woods occupied over one-half of the property. They encircled the house and the pastures like a thick horseshoe. Joe told me that these and nearby woods were once tobacco and corn fields. Human and mule energy once pushed back the trunks and vines to create open fields to plant tobacco and build a small house. Southern farmers have long since departed, their homes foreclosed during the Great Depression. Banks then divided sprawling farms into smaller geometric plots.

The woods and fields were radically altered over the course of only a couple generations. The oak trees with the thickest trunks were seedlings when Governor Huey Long was assassinated in Louisiana and Governor John Ehringhaus helped provide Depression-era farmers with access to electricity in North Carolina. Hurricanes have left uprooted trees in their wake. Torrents created by violent rains have trenched valleys winding toward the creek and these violent currents have unearthed small animal skulls, WWII-era beer bottles, rifle shells, and rocks that were buried in the late Cretaceous period. The only items that have lasted through the last century are the Civil War mounds, which Joe pointed out to me. A local history professor told Joe they were Confederate redoubts. Even they must have changed shape with erosion and burrowing animals.

Surprisingly, the rapidly changing surface of river and railroad banks was an occasion of joy and cheer for Thoreau. In the "Spring" chapter of *Walden*, he wrote that

> Few phenomena gave me more delight than to observe the forms which thawing sand and clay assume in flowing down the sides of a deep cut on the railroad through which I passed on my way to the village . . . the sand begins to flow down the slopes like lava, sometimes bursting out through the snow and overflowing it where no sand was to be seen before. Innumerable little streams overlap and interlace one with another, exhibiting a sort of hybrid product, which obeys half way the law of currents, and half way that of vegetation.

The woods also delighted Joe. Trees led his eyes upward in awe. At the forest top, a few trees struggled to claim all the sun's rays, while younger trees, typically stunted pines, seemed forever doomed to shadow. Lured by the shimmering shadows in the woods, we strayed off the path. In the absence of landmarks, all directions looked the same, which lent the place an ancient aura. My imagination conjured Arthur Dimmesdale and Hester Prynne lying among the fallen leaves, or native tribes hunting deer. Each bark had a distinct texture, and with the touch of sunlight the shades of color received a jolt of energy. The scene in the middle distance looked like a Renoir landscape, with blue shadows and dappled surfaces. It is the joy experienced by Hopkins in "Pied Beauty":

> Glory be to God for dappled things—
> For skies of couple-colour as a brinded cow;
> For rose-moles all in stipple upon trout that swim;
> Fresh-firecoal chestnut-falls; finches' wings;
> Landscape plotted and pieced—fold, fallow, and plough. . . .

But in truth a world of pain lurked in the woods. Spider webs, spanning long reaches between branches and trunks, clung to my face and arms. As I learned to my regret a few days later, chiggers and ticks lay in wait for my leg to brush against them or my head to duck under a branch. The chigger is microscopic. The tick, as small as the head of a pin, possesses an impressive miniature architecture. Haller's organs on each foreleg are vast collections of sensors and nerves, designed to detect a few molecules of carbon dioxide or a whiff of sweat. Once the complex radar system in the foreleg alerts it to an oncoming warm-blooded creature, it leaps onto its victim and burrows into the flesh. "No bird or mammal can pass near a tick," explains David George Haskell in *The Forest Unseen*, "without being detected by smell, touch, and temperature."

Dragonflies with six wings darted close, and countless biting bugs dove toward my ears. Overturned rocks revealed red, black, and white ants. Insect poisons can result in grapefruit-sized welts, unbearable itching, and neurological disease. There are 1.3 million species of insects on earth, and it seems as if half of them are in these woods. By contrast, there are only 5,400 species of mammals, 10,000 species of birds, and 15,000 species of fish. If you picture a round clock face, the clockwise sweep from 12 o'clock to 11:58 would represent insect species, with the remaining two minutes for mammals, birds, and fish.

When I returned to New York after that trip, my first stop was at an urgent care facility. Large swaths of welts had erupted on my upper thighs and around my ankles. Pain was equally distributed between a ferocious itch and pressure from liquid building up under the rash. The doctor hypothesized fungus, poison ivy, or hives and prescribed a couple of creams. Nothing eased the pain. A Southern doctor would have easily diagnosed the chigger bites I had gotten during my walk with Joe.

Those bites would inspire me to buy keets and pullets a year later. Their prowess in devouring insects would be my first line of defense against the predators that sought my skin and blood. My thoughts shifted toward egg production only several months after we acquired them. My first thought was: these birds could mow down chiggers and ticks. Their powerful neck muscles could keep their heads bobbing into the earth and around strands of vegetation for hours at a time.

The intense, tactile presence of insects was obvious to the Thoreau in his *Journal*. But *Walden* is interested more in emblems than in real insects. The minutely observed mock epic battle of the ants in "Brute Neighbors" demonstrated the violence and pointlessness of war, and the comparison of black and red ants to imperialists and colonists served only to belittle human actors. With the voracious caterpillar and the maggot in "Higher Laws," Thoreau meditated upon acquisitive humanity, for whom appetite blocks the flight of the higher faculties. "The gross feeder is a man in the larva state; and there are whole nations in that condition, nations without fancy or imagination, whose vast abdomens betray them." And the bug trapped in the sixty-year-old table at the end of "Conclusion" signaled the hope of personal resurrection, however delayed, by objects of our own making.

Thoreau was disturbed by human slumber, sloth, and greed as well as by the national will to war and industry. For my part, my walks were disturbed by persistent gnawing upon my flesh. Once, when I was clearing the creek of fallen branches, I fell backwards into the leaf-filled mud. By the time I extricated myself my wrist was welted from spider bites and wounds from several unidentified piercers.

During another episode of landscape clearing, I was chain-sawing a small tree that had grown inside an ancient stump. Balancing myself over the stump and down into the rotted depths, I wrenched my back and fell into Irish moss and Japanese stiltgrass. Unable to stand until Peri finally heard my cries for help, I suffered dozens of attacks from insects burrowing in the tangled vegetation. For a while I thought I had escaped the carnage, but alas. Some insects, such as the chigger and the seed tick, inflict liquid-filled wounds that will not appear for hours, if not days. The constant barrage of tiny puncture wounds can nudge anyone one into acarophobia—literally the fear of ticks, but psychologically the delusion that one's skin is crawling with imaginary insects.

In 1832 Charles Darwin sailed into San Salvador, Brazil, and wandered into the forests of Bahia. His journal recorded his admiration at the luxuriance of the vegetation, a sense quickly overcome by the deafening sound of insects. "The noise from the insects is so loud, that it may be heard even in a vessel anchored several hundred yards from the shore." Thirty-three years later, as Sherman marched from Georgia to North Carolina to meet Johnston at Bentonville, North Carolina, for the war's last major battle, Louis Agassiz undertook an expedition up the Amazon. It was only a few years after Darwin had published *On the Origin of Species*, and the most famous scientist in America took a steamer to Brazil to prove that the "transmutation theory," Darwin's theory of natural selection, "is wholly without foundation in fact."

A young William James accompanied his teacher on the expedition. The scientist and his student, traveling thousands of miles upstream, primarily collected fish specimens, but insects as well. Later, Agassiz published *The Classification of Insects from Embryological Data*, in which he changed the orders of insects. The previous scientific attempt at classification had arranged insects according to the extent of the metamorphosis from egg to adult animal. Agassiz thought it would be more accurate to classify insects according to how they incorporate nutrients—whether they suck or chew. Pragmatically, that is how insects interact with human beings.

At the end of *Origin of the Species,* Darwin sang a hymn to nature, proclaiming that there is a grandeur in the view of life in which teeming species have evolved from a simple beginning. Perhaps a theoretical grandeur, viewed from the study and not from the bank itself. It is foolish to walk through the woods or by the creek, however grand, without dousing your skin with eucalyptus, tea tree, and peppermint oils and spraying your clothes with permethrin. The armor of the nature lover tends to turn a walk into an armed encounter, a pasture into a field of battle. Memories of grandeur arrive post-bellum, behind screened porches and closed doors.

Plato and Churchill

We purchased our guineas just after Independence Day. They arrived in a box from Missouri. Shipped just after hatching, they had neither eaten nor pooped during their first three days of life. One had been crushed to death by her colleagues during the journey. One death per dozen is a good outcome for shipped hatchlings.

The survivors ranged in hardihood. A few spritely keets wriggled in our fingers, others were lithe but passively accepted our firm grip. One was pallid and limp. It had only hours to live—an outcome hatcheries euphemistically call failure to thrive.

One by one we dipped their beaks in water to teach them to drink. Once in a bin layered with pine shavings, they dashed around like golf balls with feet. Eating, drinking, and pooping came naturally. Like humans, they fought for no reason. The alpha picked up a pine shaving, with no nutritional value and indistinguishable from hundreds of other pine shavings, and a rugby match began. Back and forth to the corners of the bin and back, the entire flock followed one audacious demagogue.

A heat lamp hovered above the bin, replacing a mother guinea's snuggling warmth. We learned to adjust the lamp according to the keets' sleeping position—if they huddle, they are too cold; if they space themselves widely apart, they are too warm. Growth spurts occur in the Goldilocks position.

In about six weeks they were large enough to be moved to a barn stall. With only one light bulb to make them feel at home, they knew only shadows for several weeks. Finally liberated, they ventured out of the barn for a moment or two, then, in lockstep, retreated into their cave. A few weeks later still, they ventured out with more confidence. A few recently flew over the fence in the morning, and spent the rest of the day wondering how to get back. Their value is in eating the chiggers and ticks that fill the North Carolina landscape. But poop is the only constant. They poop on the beaches, they poop on the landing grounds, they poop in the fields and in the streets, they poop in the hills. But we watch them dash in teams with wonder and amusement, and they add a bit of flair to the farm.

*Evidence of Things Not Seen**

A brick path runs from our back porch to the driveway, separating the house from a trapezoidal plot in which randomly placed boulders, a few sprawling juniper bushes, and a solitary maple bestow the aura of a Japanese garden. The sparse vegetation flourishes without human intervention. Weeds do not sprout, and it is difficult to get a foothold among the rocks. At about 450 square feet (one percent of an acre), it was the only piece of my twenty-two acres that I had no plans to clear, mow, or cultivate.

One sultry summer day I trod along the path, a shovel in one hand and tractor keys in the other, creating a mental list of morning chores. I was startled from my reverie by the squawking of a guinea hen (a confusing term, as it can refer to either gender). He perched on one of the larger rocks, balanced on one leg, shooting me an angry glare. It is not unusual to see a solitary guinea in a tree or on a roof; a flock of guineas typically appoints a guard, who sounds the alarm upon spotting a looming hawk or human. A solitary guinea on a rock, however, is an unusual sight.

I carefully zig-zagged among the boulders, determined to see what he was protecting. Upon my approach, the guard guinea stalked off in a huff. The rock forma-

**Hebrews* 11:1

tion he had abandoned formed a small cave. I stared down into the cave opening and saw nothing. But crouching down, I spotted two dozen eggs piled further inside. (Guinea hens are notorious for hiding their eggs.) There is no mistaking a guinea egg for a chicken egg. It is smaller and more obloid (the rounder bottom curves more quickly to the other, pointier end, rather like a teardrop). The shell is harder, and the color is a flatter white. And it is usually harder for predators to find. Typically, once guineas select a hiding spot, several hens lay their eggs, one female is appointed to brood, and one male is appointed to stand guard. The female must have been stretching her legs. Studying the pyramid of eggs, I smiled in admiration over the patience and fortitude of the guard.

For several days I honored the privacy of the nest. But I soon noticed the guineas no longer hung around the garden. Leaders of the flock still squawked to warn their kin about my wandering Dobermans or circling hawks, but now from trees in distant pastures. I was suspicious and walked to the nesting spot. I knelt before the opening in the rocks and peered in disbelief into a void. Not a single egg remained. As I stared in disbelief, my mind went vacant and my limbs froze. Then mental paralysis yielded to confusion.

When my brain fired up again, I tried to piece together a string of observations, using an amateur form of Bayesian logic—following probable paths, having identified likely starting points: The keets had not hatched, as there were no broken shells. The guineas had abandoned their post. I had recently noticed two translucent skins that copperheads had shed. I had also recently noticed a black snake behind the barn with an ovoid object working its way down its throat. Guineas can kill snakes (they circle the snake, then rush in for the kill), but I had kept the flock locked in the barn at night, when snakes are on the prowl. Therefore, a snake (or perhaps a family of snakes) must have recently slithered away having feasted on guinea eggs. Many other possible predators exist—hawks, falcons, owls, foxes, raccoons, frogs, large mice—but nothing seemed as logical as the snake scenario.

Much of what happens on the farm goes unnoticed, at least by me. Hawks kill domesticated fowl; turtles dig holes; woodchucks nibble at bushes; deer tease our dogs from beyond the fence. I see the results but can never be sure of the cause. I am not as skeptical as the philosopher Hume, who claimed that since there is no sense impression that links cause and effect, we cannot know with certainty that the sun will rise tomorrow. I am, however, burdened with the unsettling feeling that certainty is beyond my grasp. Uncertainty is a structural feature of being human, and anxiety seeps into our consciousness unbidden: Will my course of study yield a satisfying career? Will the person with whom I've fallen in love remain a life partner? When and how will I die?

Musing on the missing guinea eggs, I concluded that life on the farm has intensified the feeling of uncertainty. I can only struggle to achieve what Keats two centuries ago called negative capability, the ability to accept uncertainties, mysteries, and doubts. The best I can do as a detective is to discover what is probable. It is a humble philosophical position. Nature is always at least a couple of steps ahead of me.

Nothing New Under the Sun

On a cool evening I spent an hour trying to urge the guineas into the barn. I flanked them, arms swinging wildly, but they scattered. Some stood still, out of reach, while others fluttered about. A few ran inside, apparently by mistake. While I hustled after others, the birds within the barn walked single file back outside to join their recalcitrant colleagues.

Determined to spend the night outdoors, they perched on boughs, lurching from one branch to a higher one until they reached a height beyond the jaws of four-legged predators but within easy reach of winged ones. Sometimes they fluttered back into the barn unbidden and perched on the highest rafters. I put straw on one side of the wall, hoping that their droppings would land there. They perched such that the gravity would direct the poop onto the straw. But the next morning I scraped fallen poop from the other side of the wall. A thought flickered in my mind—perhaps I can turn the birds around. But that is a Sisyphean task. And after noting that my mind had come up with an original, if impossible, plan, I stumbled across a stanza from Shelby Stephenson's poem "Joshua Lee Said":

> I had a friend poorer than I was:
> chickens roosted on the well-curb
> and his job was to go out

and turn them birds around
so their droppings would hit the ground.

The notion of shifting the trajectory of chicken poop exhilarated me. A simple poem deflated me. I should have been warned by *Ecclesiastes*: "Is there anything of which it may be said, 'See, this *is* new'? It has already been in ancient times before us."

There is an old story that philosophers used to climb a mountain to find wisdom at the summit. Struggling with metaphysical or epistemological problems on the ascent, they would encounter Plato on his way back down. A neophyte farmer, I am the dull philosopher of derivative wisdom. Powerless to direct the fall of guinea poop onto straw, I am resigned to scraping walls, and to unoriginal thoughts.

Barnyard Economics

During harvest season the Orange County paper listed farms showing off their produce, animals, and wares. Peri's imagination focused on an alpaca farm, so we drove northward on narrow roads that curved gently toward the South American transplants. The car crawled up a long dirt driveway that bordered several acres of pasture and grazing beasts. We greeted the farming couple. Under a tent, the husband explained how they milked and sheared the flock, and showed us the soaps and weavings they sold. The flare from Peri's eyes told me we were in imminent danger of purchasing alpacas. I was relieved when the farmer's wife began explaining details of animal husbandry, and how much expertise was required to address twisted intestines, difficult births, and other medical complications.

A few dozen chickens roamed outside the herd's fence. The red, green, and black flare of a rooster's tail feathers caught Peri's attention, and she barraged the farmers with questions about chickens and eggs. We had recently discussed raising chickens to put our land to good use, help reduce the bug population, and produce our own eggs. If we wanted to purchase chicks, they told us, we should visit Steven, a bird enthusiast in a nearby town who raised hundreds of varieties of fowl.

A few weeks later, we went to investigate. We drove a dozen miles northwest on dusty roads, past dense woods and vast farmland. Houses were buried deep within the woods, with no addresses visible from the road. We drove up a few driveways and knocked on doors until at last one elderly woman pointed us to the property of the "chicken man."

As we drove into the woods toward his house, the path became hedged with cages and coops filled with peacocks, ducks, a colorful array of parrots, and dozens of varieties of chickens. Being cooped is not fun for the birds but has advantages over letting them roam for the farmer. First, caged birds are protected from hawks, owls, and raccoons. Second, valuable species are kept pure. Third, poop is easily scooped.

Finally, it is easy for first-time purchasers to explore at leisure and observe exotic coloring and curious sideways glances. We drifted among the cages for the next hour admiring the youthful playfulness of the birds. Peri remained silent, imagining which varieties would fill our barn and grace our pastures.

We returned to the house to discuss our options. Steven was a collector more than a business owner, but was happy to help locals start their own flocks. He helped Peri select three varieties. The next step was to choose the pullets, or female chicks.

My father spent a few childhood years in Chania, a city on the northwest coast of Crete. Toward the end of his life, he told me that his parents put him in charge of the chickens. His mother, he once reminisced, had an unerring sense of chicken gender. She would cup a chick, turn it over, blow gently on the fluff, and separate the males from the females. Nowadays, however, that expertise seems to be lost. Steven picked up a series of lavender Orpingtons, particularly cute, cuddly, and colorful chicks, and promised us six pullets. A few months later, we discovered that five were roosters, and particularly ill-natured roosters at that. Because there is a pecking order on the farm, their sex was a death sentence. To avoid giving them the literal hatchet, we gave them away to a few friends whose flocks needed male protection or fertilization services.

Peri named the remaining male Albert, the first of many chickens to be baptized with names of English royalty. Albert's alpha position now unquestioned, he threw out his chest further with every growth spurt. It is popularly believed that roosters crow at dawn, but that is a half-truth. Roosters *begin* crowing at dawn. Ours was particularly boastful, crowing long past sunrise. He was also incredibly daring. After a few months, he began lunging at Peri whenever she approached the pasture. Fear of the beast's animosity kept her on alert, and she must have felt like the young David Copperfield beset by farmyard arrogance: "There is one cock who gets upon a post to crow, and seems to take particular notice of me as I look at him through the kitchen window, who makes me shiver, he is so fierce."

A sentimental animal lover, Peri simply yelled at him, and once gave him a diminutive kick. But the bullying continued. As an alpha male protector of my harem of one, I threw myself into the fray. When the reprobate ran toward me, I stood my ground and waited for his arrival. When he got close enough, I swooped my leg into him. I imagined myself kicking a field goal, but Albert barely budged. His chest muscle was several pounds of quartz hiding under fluffy lavender feathers, and my boot bounced off him. Undeterred, the rooster hurled himself at me once more, and I rewarded his stubbornness with a sideways swipe. He has henceforth avoided looking directly at me and swerves upon my approach.

An exotic rooster can host a spectacular array of brightly colored feathers. He can also alert the rest of the flock to intruders from above (hawks), below (snakes), and in between (foxes and raccoons). But if your goal is eggs, roosters are useless. As a result of a utilitarian calculation—dollars spent on feed minus egg laying value equals a waste of money—over 200 million cockerels, or male chicks, are killed every year. They are ground alive, suffocated, or fed to snakes.

Steven's home was tucked away in the woods. In his spare time, he amassed volumes of information about birds and a collection of exotic species. He offered us lots of advice about raising chicks and we remained friends. After our initial purchase, however, we began to order chicks from hatcheries because we wanted our flock inoculated against coccidiosis and Marek's disease. Because our hatcheries are located in Missouri and Iowa, the chicks are delivered in boxes, having been selected and sexed at birth. They are left unfed until they arrive so that their intestines are not awakened. As with our guineas, one or two tend to suffocate or are crushed to death by their peers along the way. Given heat and nourishment, most of them thrive. Besides starter feed, what they seem to like best is hard-boiled eggs.

Chicks peep even before they hatch. Once dashing around, creating their bird hierarchies and eating their weight in grain, they are said to make thirty distinct sounds, signifying everything from panic to pleasure. From their first day on earth what they do best is create a mess, fouling their water and food with pine shavings and worse. I believe primitive peoples intuited the second law of thermodynamics by observing chickens. Entropy is the law in chicken coops and wherever they may roam. An orderly pile of leaves becomes a scattered mess whenever a chicken appears, a clean watering bowl is soon littered, and a manicured lawn is swiftly turned into a succession of scratched-out holes. A gentleman's farm obeys all the laws of thermodynamics, and I here present them in Pynchon's paraphrase for the non-physicist. First, you can't win. Second, things are going to get worse before they get better. Third, who says they're going to get better?*

I know of two liturgical ways to follow a strict daily schedule. Christian monks who follow the Roman Breviary or the Greek Horologion pray at prescribed times, such as matins at midnight, prime at 6 am, and vespers at 6 pm. Priests perform the liturgy at defined hours. The muezzin, on the other hand, calls worshipers to prayer from his minaret five times each day, according to the position of astronomical bodies. Chickens are more like Muslims than Christians. Tending to them coincides with the earth's rotation. There is a sense of urgency, even moral responsibility, in both prayer and tending your flock. Lest I be accused of heresy, however, I am quick to admit the theological distance between prayer and feeding. Feeding is more mindless repetition than ritual, and if I fail, I risk not damnation but fewer eggs for me and discomfort and hunger for the chickens.

*From Pynchon's short story "Entropy"

After a season, chicks become hens and begin to lay. Ours began their laying responsibilities in early spring. Each day I make my first walk to the barn at sunrise. The rooster has begun to crow, and piles of poop have collected overnight. Scraping the perches is the first order of business. Scraping clears the way to the feeders, helps prevent salmonella, and keeps noxious odors from overwhelming the senses and attracting germs and insects.

Next, I return to the house to exercise, eat breakfast, and read newspapers and emails. Then it's back to the barn to distribute crackle, the daily treat for adult chickens. For the adolescents, like any good parent, I make sure their water is sufficient. Then I collect eggs, so that the next layer won't crush them or a snake won't swallow them.

Hens lay sequentially throughout the morning and afternoon, taking turns in the nesting boxes or in hiding places around the property. A hen will cluck for five minutes after laying her egg. I enjoy yelling at them: "What do you want, a medal?" If they were contemporary children, they would get one.

Our chickens are free range or, more accurately, pasture fed, which makes for tastier eggs with less cholesterol and saturated fat and more vitamin A and E, beta carotene, and omega-3 fatty acids. But being free-range risks being taken by overhead predators. Adult chickens are too large for a hawk or falcon to hoist away, but nothing will hinder the killing instinct. I once saw a falcon feast on a bird more than twice its size. When I approached, it tried to lift its prey to safety. Failing to budge it, it escaped empty-clawed.

Smaller chicks are hawk appetizers, so we keep them

in a cage inside the barn until they are almost fully grown. That requires constant feeding, more trips to the barn, and cleaning in awkward spots. They also soil their food and water for sport, so the returns to the barn become dizzying. The payoff comes when the hens begin to lay. We now have four generations of chickens—adults, adolescents, children, and infants. Starting with a small handful, the flock grew to fifty, then one hundred. From a couple of eggs per day we now receive three or four dozen. When the next generations come online, we'll collect a few dozen more.

It's not easy to calculate the profit from selling a dozen eggs. The cost of pullets ranges among common and exotic breeds. The life span of a hen is random: she might be crushed to death in her delivery box; she might fail to thrive, her growth spurts slowing until she expires; a predator might carry her off; she might brood for a period until she resumes her reproductive responsibilities; she might simply cease laying eggs ahead of schedule. Nevertheless, the government demands an accounting, and I am curious about the financial returns of all my scooping, feeding, and tending. I am almost as scrupulous as E. B. White, who noted his chicken and egg expenses down to the second decimal in *One Man's Meat*. My results are just as shocking. The table on the next page shows the annual costs before a single egg is laid.

After the initial investment, you can make a rough calculation of profits by estimating how many eggs your flock will produce in a year. This is tricky, as very few eggs are laid when the thermometer peaks at 106 degrees (in a stuffy barn) or dips into the single digits. But on

Cost of 50 pullets, including immunization and shipping	$225
4 bales of barley straw (good for four months)	$64
Fine gravel for barn drainage	$350
Waterers and feeders	$65
Water heating element	$40
Corn (scratch)	$92
Layer feed	$149
Roosting poles	$45
Nesting boxes	$37
	$1,067

average a hen will lay two eggs every three days, or two hundred and forty per year. The pullets took six months to start laying, so our flock should have yielded five hundred dozen eggs. But hawks get hungry, and chickens are prone to respiratory and cloacal infections as well as tumors, so production fell to about three hundred and fifty dozen. A local farm cooperative offered us $3 per dozen, so we grossed $1,050. Thus, we ended the year in the red. If we had amortized the barn and the land each dozen would have cost us $350.

I find it puzzling to observe the chickens rush toward me when I approach the barn. Their quick, choreographed gait gives the impression of impending joy at my arrival. But just as they get within hugging distance, they stop short, eye me suspiciously, and scatter, as if I come looking for my evening meal. I'm the one who keeps their feeders full, treats them with corn at dawn, and sanitizes their roost. Are they blessed with short memories or are they simply ungrateful? But then again, they see me snatch their unborn every time I enter the barn.

My anxieties are echoed in the burst of farm-related resentments of Mr. Thompson in *Noon Wine*, the central novel in Katherine Anne Porter's trilogy *Pale Horse, Pale Rider*:

> Hens worried him, cackling, clucking, hatching out when you least expected it and leading their brood into the barnyard where the horses could step on them; dying of roup and wryneck and getting plagues of chicken lice; laying eggs all over God's creation so that half of them were spoiled before a man could find them, in spite of a rack of nests Mrs. Thompson had set out for them in the feed room. Hens were a blasted nuisance.

Aside from the annoying daily behaviors of domesticated fowl, Mr. Thompson was bedeviled by shame, as the community considered attending to chickens to be a female duty.

The final call to prayer in the daily life of our chickens comes at dusk. In my evening walk to the barn, I turn off the light and close the barn door. With only a few moments of daylight remaining, it is impossible to herd chickens into the barn. Cooing, yelling, running with arms outstretched, or staring with a puritanical glare will only cause renegade chickens to flee. The birds and I are like two north magnetic poles. Only when it is sufficiently dark will all the birds have found their roosting spot.

Without malice, older birds, roosting above the babies in their cage, poop on them. Chicks below scramble, but they are as helpless as a prisoner in the crypt of a medieval castle, the baron on the floor above. If you want to show the prisoner who is in charge, the great and stately medieval scholar Peter Brown once declared in a lecture, shit on them. Eliot captured this degraded and bathetic sense that poop evokes in the final stanza of "Sweeney among the Nightingales." Birds (not chickens, but more elegant, melodic, and elegiac nightingales) soiled Agamemnon's garment when Clytemnestra murdered him in his bath:

> And sang within the bloody wood
> When Agamemnon cried aloud,
> And let their liquid siftings fall
> To stain the stiff dishonoured shroud.

I do not know what happens in the barn once the door is shut tight. A snake might enter, but there are no eggs by then, and chickens consider them, quite logically, to be large worms. For the most part, there is quiet in the barn, although once one squawk is heard a symphony follows. Quiet eventually returns, and a few restful hours later the cycle begins again.

Sunny Side Up

The moment I shoved open the porch door, a pre-dawn winter wind sucker punched me. The ground crunched beneath my boots as I made my way to the barn. Just above the horizon, the sun splashed the eastern sky orangey-pink. The air smelled of ice and trees. As I pulled the henhouse door open enough to peek inside, odors of straw and warmth and manure assaulted me.

I kept the door slightly ajar, preventing the normal chaotic rush to the fields. Hens collide like heated atoms. Aggrieved, they fluttered and grumbled as I took the morning census. Four Heritage Barred Rock, five Lavender, and four Black Copper Maran chickens, heads cocked sideways, stared back at me. Seven White African and nine Royal Purple guineas blinked and fussed. No overnight predators had decreased the flock. I opened the barn door fully after they paraded past me, and I entered the barn to collect some manure in a bucket and fluff a bit of wheat straw.

The repetitive scraping of poop began to numb my mind. But then a ray of morning sunlight drew my eyes to a small brown elliptical orb camouflaged in the straw. Then another. For a moment I seemed to lose consciousness: my breathing stopped and the barn disappeared. Our first eggs gradually came into focus. I was not prepared for this discovery. Neighbors had warned me that young hens would not start laying in the midst of winter. Our babies were rebels.

For these two eggs, small as ping pong balls, we had held the chicks every day, kept them warm in fresh pine shavings, supplied them with medicated starter feed. We had invested hundreds of pounds and dollars and hours. But as quickly as the calculations flooded my mind, my heart released them. A breathless joy overtook the scrupulous accounting.

For the first time on the farm, I realized the distance I had traveled from a dense, urban environment. I was witnessing a miracle of everyday farm life. For me, at that moment, it was a brave new world, that had such wonders in it. I realized I was sitting in the midst of irrepressible natural forces. I had a childlike reaction to nature's wonders. They are as surprising as they are commonplace. I recalled Olmsted's vision, when contemplating Central Park in Manhattan and Prospect Park in Brooklyn, that even a brief retreat into a natural setting would rejuvenate us, repair the damage that intense urban environments inflict upon us, invite us to meditate, and restore the vitality and mental health that underwrite citizens' participation in America's experiment in civic democracy.

Then a moment of bathos, as I noticed the eggs were nestled in the straw along with the usual dollops of chicken poop. Augustine's unusually anatomical pronouncement sprung to mind: we are all born between urine and feces. Or, as Yeats's Crazy Jane says to the Bishop, "But Love has pitched his mansion in the place of excrement."

I flicked bits of poop from the shells and cradled the two miniature eggs in one hand. On my way back to the house to surprise Peri, the eggs put my psychological drama in perspective. Stuck inside my head, I had thought that my pendulum swings between melancholy and joy were part of a distressed mind. Chickens and eggs invited me to look at the farm from a cosmic perspective—I saw myself as an infinitely small creature in nature, where loss and rebirth mingled. By the time I reached the house the surge of joy that rushed me in the barn had modulated into calm meditation. I opened my palm, and Peri and I shared a moment of quiet wonder.

Anatomical Footnote

Humans may be born between urine and feces, as Augustine reminds us, but chickens are not. This took me a long time to figure out, as I was determined to solve a problem with observation alone: why have I never seen a chicken pee. I followed chickens while they tore across pastures, scratched leaves and dirt patches, and nestled. My experiment failed, until I yielded to my academic impulses. In my research into chicken urine, I discovered that chickens technically do not urinate because they do not have bladders. That organ is relatively heavy, and evolution has determined that flight is more important than a urinary tract and all its accoutrements. For proof, I offer Hurston's folksy aphorism in *Their Eyes Were Watching God*: "Chicken drink water, but he don't pee-pee." When birds produce uric acid it flows into the cloaca, where it meets digestive waste. The end result is poop topped with urine, brown dollops with a white frosting. It is the loose whitewash with which drivers are all too familiar.

Survival of the Fittest

I tried to scrape the chicken droppings with a trowel, but they had frozen onto the roosts. I twisted the bronze nozzle to fill the waterers, but the hose had solidified. While cracking the ice, I heard one hen squawk and another reply. Soon hens in a dozen nesting boxes joined the conversation. The loudest of chicken sounds is not the rooster crowing but the hen complaining or boasting. Having sat quietly for part of the morning in their nesting boxes, their squawking erupted. This disturbing noise, blasted in a minor key, announced the laying of an egg. Creating a yolk, surrounding it with a calcium shell, and coloring it on the journey through the oviduct and the cloaca, consumes a lot of energy. In that sub-zero February morning the hens earned the right to trumpet their strident song. I suspected they needed to communicate to their maternal peers that they had done their bit for the continuation of the species. I also feared that they had unwittingly communicated to egg predators that their next meal had just been served.

After circumnavigating the globe and tracking species from spiders to finches, Darwin discovered that species adapted to their environment to survive. Mendel's discovery of genetic inheritance laid the groundwork for the idea that genes could mutate, which supplied the means of evolutionary adaptation. Later still, biologists and anthropologists showed that genes could control communal and self-sacrificial behavior as well as survival mechanisms, such as camouflage, posture, and brain size.

This trajectory of intuition, hypothesis, and experimentation seemed like science fiction around the barn. So many animal behaviors seemed destined for extinction. The morning annunciation ritual of hens was a primary example of this counter-intuitive behavior on our farm, made even more confusing when mothers often abandoned their unborn offspring for a day of scratching for insects. The vast majority of eggs were left without heat or protection. With mothers like that, it's hard to imagine how this species has perpetuated itself.

After establishing our small flock of chickens, Peri decided that some of our pastures needed grazing animals. I researched various species to populate our new farmland—sheep, donkeys, alpaca—but Peri argued that a herd of goats could best mow pastures and clear the woods of thorny and poisonous vines. The myotonic goat in particular caught her attention. When confronted by a predator, this animal faints. More precisely, it loses muscle control, not consciousness, temporarily, but long enough to be gobbled by a coyote. Why hasn't this genetic modification been cauterized? Polyvagal theory explains that this passive response to primitive neurological functions takes over the brain during times of extreme stress. But a hungry predator would not likely wait for the myotonic brain to awaken. In any case, when we discovered the extent of the fencing and medical expertise this venture required, we abandoned all hope.

Not to be outdone, chickens have an even more debilitating sleep pattern. The dozing chicken resembles a patient in a catatonic stupor. I once came upon a rooster, prostrate and half buried in wheat straw in the corner of the barn, and I thought his spirit had transpired over the course of the snowy afternoon. As I didn't want the dozen feathered bipeds scurrying around the barn to get depressed, I slowly attempted to remove the carcass. It was warm but motionless. Recently deceased, I thought. But it slowly raised its beak, craning its neck toward me with an angry scowl. It was not dead, but in such a deep sleep that it would have been easy prey for a snake, raccoon, or hawk. When I am late locking the chickens in the barn at night, and they are sleeping on bales of straw, it is near impossible to wake them. One must carefully wrap both hands around their girth and whisk them away before their wings flutter in resistance.

Last summer, our guineas produced two large piles of eggs. When the first batch hatched, the adults herded the keets away from us toward a row of abelia bushes. When we tried to urge the new parents into the barn, we were greeted with hostile glares and aggressive screams. One female spread her wings over two dozen hatchlings and settled down for the night. The wingspan resembled Renaissance paintings of Mary spreading her blue mantle over a congregation, and my anxiety was softened by this instinctive act of protection. But the next morning Peri discovered a pile of two dozen expired keets, crushed and suffocated.

The next batch seemed off to a better start. Twenty-two keets scampered off with two adults, who mimicked how to scratch the earth and dip their beaks into the soil. The next day I counted only twenty. The next day sixteen. The adults seemed unconcerned as the flock whittled down to the single digits. During the week of the missing keets, Peri heard a soft peeping in one of the barn stalls. I noticed a small hole with a beak peeking out of fine dirt. I could fit only one finger in the hole but managed to scoop up one of the missing babies. Exploring deeper into the hole, I managed to excavate three others. Peri collected the abandoned four and we brought them to a bin equipped with a warming lamp and nourishment. They were the only keets hatched in the two piles of eggs that summer to survive into adulthood.

The Darwin Award is typically given to individuals who eliminate themselves in an extraordinarily idiotic manner. If animals could win a Darwin Award, there would be many contenders: deer that cross the highway against a red light; copperheads that sun themselves on country roads; blue jays that collide into our large picture window to receive a fatal concussion. But for disproving evolution's central theory, I would give the bronze to myotonic goats, the silver to chickens, and the gold to guineas.

*Carrion Comfort**

I awoke to the sound of branches cracking and crashing to the ground. Outside, the trees were drooping with ice. The glare of snow shuttered my eyes. Wrapping myself with layers of flannels and sweatshirts until they felt like swaddling clothes, I had just enough leeway to wield a chainsaw to clear the driveway and a few paths of fallen branches.

Winter is the cruelest season for trees. In our first January on the farm, I saw trunks crack at mid-height, the top portion dangling, precariously attached by a few strands of bark and fiber. Limbs matted with jade-tinted fungus fell almost as frequently as leaves. The weight of clinging ice took down massive branches. I roamed the woods weekly to clear the ground. The larger trunks I attacked with a chainsaw. Even a small tree requires a dozen cuts.

Bending over a small but wiry cedar branch, holding the saw in a precarious squatting position for several minutes, I wrenched my lower back muscles beyond their elastic limits. I was out of commission for a couple of weeks. But the falling branches kept piling. Left untended for a season, they will render the forest floor impassable. Muscles are a wasting asset, and I am gambling on how many years, or perhaps months, of strength

*Title of a Gerard Manley Hopkins poem

remain in my biceps and torso before the woods revert to chaos. Thoughts like this lead me all too easily to melancholy and depression.

At the darkest end of my emotional spectrum lurks despair. Despair is not a simple emotion, but a volatile mixture of self-pity, lack of social engagement, a break in the continuum that links humans and the natural world, a plunge in motivation and energy, and a lack of confidence in one's resilience. It is the willingness to change the narrative mode in which one has been acting, from the heroic or romantic to the lower mimetic forms of irony or farce. As an allegorical creature, despair has inhabited murky literary caves, as in Spenser's *Faerie Queene*, or gothic castles with forbidding dungeons, as in Bunyan's *Pilgrim's Progress*. Trapped in my figurative cave or dungeon, I can also feel a perverse pleasure in captivity, as Hopkins sonnet taught us: "Not, I'll not, carrion comfort, Despair, not feast on thee; not untwist—slack they may be—these last strands of man in me or, most weary cry, *I can no more*."

Winter made my spirit vulnerable to this crippling emotion. My every good intention was threatened by a sudden equal and opposite reaction in nature. I had planted pastures with buckwheat only to see the seeds washed downstream in a fierce thunderstorm—which took with it a few inches of fertile earth for good measure. Hawks and raccoons threatened to decimate, or entirely ravage, our flock of hens. Months of tending, feeding, cleaning, and watering could be wasted in an instant, and a considerable investment in egg production would fall into negative territory.

I experienced nothing of the magnitude of loss felt

by farmers in the great dust bowl of the Southern Plains or the brutal winters of the Northern Plains. I did not compare myself to the emaciated farmhands photographed in James Agee and Walker Evans's *Let Us Now Praise Famous Men* or the immigrant homesteaders who struggle in South Dakota's sunbaked and snow-blasted fields in Edith Eudora Kohl's *Land of the Burnt Thigh.* My survival was not at stake, perhaps just my mental stability. I often found myself staring into the existential abyss. And that way madness lies. As Nietzsche warned, "He who fights with monsters should be careful lest he thereby becomes a monster. And if thou gaze long into an abyss, the abyss will also gaze into thee."

The twentieth-century novelist most obsessed with the abyss was Nietzsche's disciple, Nikos Kazantzakis, whose *The Saviors of God: Spiritual Exercises* begins with the haunting sentence: "We come from a dark abyss, we end in a dark abyss, and we call the luminous interval life." I was not searching for philosophical or theological truths on the farm. I was simply trying to prove to myself that my muscles will not slack, that my research can keep up with the complexities of chicken diseases and the soil's chemical and bacterial composition, and that I will eventually see clover sprout or eggs laid.

But my back inevitably tore. I remained dumb in the face of nature's challenges, as trees collapsed and the reproductive cycles of flora and fauna failed. Hopkins extricated himself from despair by wrestling with his God. But I am no Jacob, nor was meant to be.* As I lay

*After T. S. Eliot's poem "The Love Song of J. Alfred Prufrock"

paralyzed, with electric shocks wreaking havoc in my lower back and down my thighs, I did not embark on a theodicy. I simply stared into the abyss.

Repetition

One chilly autumn night I dreamt of chickens lined atop roosts. They were joyfully releasing streams of waste. The nightmare continued as I watched poop pile into pyramids on the barn floor. I awoke envisioning the task of poop removal that awaited me. The daily cloacal cycle of chicken waste evacuation had sadly been permanently etched on my psyche. Chicken poop has become my Swiftian scatological obsession on the farm.

I trudged to the barn at sunrise with only half of my brain neurons firing, just enough to power me to the trowels and shovels I had cleaned, and buckets that I had emptied, the day before. Slowly making my way from the back porch to the barn, I kicked droppings of the previous day from the cement pavement into soil. Arriving at the barn, I opened the door as dozens of cackling birds dashed past my boots, tripping over each other to escape their befouled dungeon.

Once in the barn, I gazed with stupefaction at the random placement of poop. Thus began my morning ritual. I scraped poop from ledges, which were stained with brown and white drips. Gripping my trowel, I stretched one arm under two roosts to fling poop into a bucket, which I held with the other arm. The barn stall formerly housed a horse, so a significant amount of poop had fallen behind the kick plates overnight. I have yet to devise a tool that will go behind, then down into the kick plate while keeping my hands unsoiled. The poop gathered in the straw was tricky as well—flicking pellets and balls of fecal matter is delicate when they are entwined. It was easier to gather the straw-poop combination, which makes a potent organic fertilizer. That strategy only delayed more work, however, as the chickens, having emerged into the daylight, sought out the piles of manure to scratch for food or burrow into.

Having purged my little Augean stables, I refilled feeding troughs, rinsed and topped up the water dispensers, and freshened the straw. I have followed these steps a few hundred times, and past is prologue to future months and years. The burden of repetition weighs heavily on my soul.

What is surprising is how quickly repetition can sap the joy out of momentary perceptions of beauty, or how deeply boredom can dull the sense of miracle apparent in the production of every egg and the bursting forth of every new blossom.

Returning from the barn I stopped by the garage to pick up my leaf blower. Leaves had piled up on the driveway and paths since I had cleared them two days ago. Danni, my female Doberman, all the while munching on poop in the pasture, turned her attention to me. Any machine got her adrenaline pumping, and she dashed toward me as I yanked on the starter rope. Barking furiously, she tried to warn me of the danger of hoisting a forty-pound backpack that made such a racket over my shoulders. I plodded across six-inch piles of oak and maple leaves, waving the blower until my carpal tunnel seized my forearm muscles. Having cleared a few hundred yards of asphalt and concrete, I felt a sense of accomplishment, followed by a sense of futility. I had repeated the chore dozens of times over the past few weeks.

That autumn I blew leaves from the patio and driveway every few days, shoveled acorns every week, and chain sawed fallen limbs monthly. Autumn tasks made me feel caught in endless loops of computer code. Locals have their own name for a project that appears to be continuous, that offers no sense of accomplishment, and that only in rare and illusory moments seems to approach the goal line. They call it "a process."

Whenever my stone mason, my contractor, my source for exotic chickens, or my southern neighbors have tried to sympathize with me—as they acknowledge the endless downpour of leaves or the infinite supply of invasive weeds or the endless production of chicken poop—they invariably respond with the same axiom. "It's a process" is a rote phrase that means "nature wins." "Sisyphean" is another term for what the locals mean—a person tortured by a task that is psychologically and physically numbing, meaningless, and without end. Sometimes I prefer the mathematical term "asymptotic": a curve that approaches the finish line but will never touch it.

It is not a brilliant insight that the landscape and animals require work. It is common farm sense. And it has been common literary sense for millennia. Pastoral and georgic works of literature, from Hesiod and Virgil to Willa Cather and Thoreau, have been concerned with shepherds tending flocks and farmers raising crops—mind-numbing, repetitive work that predictably follows daily and annual patterns.

This sort of drudgery, the dark side of virtuous, puritanical hard work, formed the background of John Williams's *Stoner*, perhaps the saddest novel of the twentieth century. William Stoner grew up in a "lonely household . . . bound together by the necessity of its toil." His parents were dirt farmers, predecessors of the poverty-stricken farmers of the Great Depression familiar to us in John Steinbeck's *Grapes of Wrath*. At his mother's funeral, William silently eulogized his parents' lives: they barely prospered from barren soil, they expended their lives in cheerless labor, and they merely endured feeling trapped and numbed.

As for the son, the muscular habits of daily toil were so enervating that it emotionally disabled him. As an adult, Stoner suffered both in love and in his career. At home, his marriage is a disaster, and he is estranged from his daughter. At the university, he is unbeloved, his work is more mechanical than inspired, and he is ultimately forgotten. Even a redemptive, transcendent love affair fails to flourish, due to the interference of a vicious colleague. Although he endured a dead-end career on a college campus and not on a farm, he inherited the fate of his parents: a long-suffering life of drudgery, loneliness, and stoic endurance.

There is no deep psychological process underlying repetition. Freud may have been right that compulsively reenacting one's trauma is the cause of repetition, but causes and effects are simpler on the farm. The fact that I am compulsive helps drive me to repeat the tasks that nature imposes upon me. Kierkegaard was closer to the truth: repetition dulls the pleasure of an act and leads to boredom.

It was boredom, anomie, and despair that afflicted Walker Percy's hero Binx Bolling in *The Moviegoer* (I describe his dilemma in the chapter "Road Trips, Southern Style: Third Meditation," below). His quest was to escape this existential morass, which he described as "everydayness." "Everydayness is the enemy. No search is possible. Perhaps there was a time when everydayness was not too strong, and one could break its grip by brute strength. Now nothing breaks it—but disaster." The mundane was a personal and cultural black hole from which nothing could escape. And in this quest novel, the physical journey was ironically rendered useless: "the everydayness is everywhere now, having begun in the cities and seeking out the remotest nooks and corners of the countryside, even the swamps."

Everydayness and boredom have been the constant features of farm life, interrupted only sporadically with what Wordsworth called spots of time, T.S. Eliot called still points in a turning world, and Woolf called moments of being. There is one glimmer of hope, however, in the mundane fact of repetition. Repetition allows for an odd sort of psychological escape from everydayness, an insight that Percy's Binx Bolling borrows from Kierkegaard. When two identical episodes bookend long periods of boredom or drudgery, the repetition will relieve the intervening time interval of its boredom and redeem it. "What is a repetition?" asked Binx. "A repetition is the re-enactment of past experience toward the end of isolating the time segment which has lapsed in order that it, the lapsed time, can be savored of itself and without the usual adulteration of events that clog time like peanuts in brittle."

But to return to earth, and to the rapidly repetitive moments of work. Repetition combats feelings of the sublime. It lowers the uplifted heart to the more earthly view of the picturesque, and further still to the mundane. The body feels the quantum downward leaps of energy levels as imaginative joy climbs down, rung by rung, to boredom and the despair of endless tedium. As the narrator of Robert Penn Warren's *A Place To Come To* says of his youth, "For many years, I could, literally, remember nothing except the repetitions of life . . . like a somnambulist wandering a dark house."

There are psychological and philosophical escape routes. For Freud, therapeutic work might reveal the original trauma, which in turn might lessen the need to repeat it. For Kierkegaard, rising from the aesthetic to the ethical, and ultimately to the religious level offers a release from pleasure-seeking repetition. But on the farm the escape routes are less lofty. Lactic acid, which builds up in working muscles and weakens them, puts a limit on mechanical tasks. I can do hard work these days for only about three hours, down from eight or nine a few decades ago. And each ten-degree rise in feverish temperature lowers my limit by an addition half hour. I can shovel stones only so long before one side of the back feels about to pull or my grip loosens. Sooner or later, I must turn from one sort of tedium to another. Shoveling rocks yields to sowing seeds or blowing leaves, which require different combinations of muscles. There is no spiritual uplift or relief in boredom, but if you alternate tasks, you might get a refreshing sense that you can mentally juggle the demands of the landscape.

And intellectual milestones also accompany the exercise of continual brute force. First, I can reassure myself that work, even tedious work, is necessary to counter the relentless entropy, chaos, and sloppiness of nature. Second, as a devotee of Cotton Mather and Ben Franklin, I might think that hard work is ethically virtuous. Third, a moment of rest might inspire a calm and contemplative glance at the beauty of a creek, a sloping pasture, or a budding tree. I've had a remarkable outburst from George Eliot's *Mill on the Floss* bouncing around in my head for four decades, a phrase that redeems the curse of boredom and connects it firmly to love: "What novelty is worth that sweet monotony where everything is known and loved because it is known."

This sentiment, the feeling that glorifies the everydayness of the world and the endless cycle of tasks, appears in the joyful chorus of the traditional Southern folk song "Cornbread and Butterbeans." Work, eat, make love, then repeat.

> Cornbread and butterbeans and you across the table
> Eatin' beans and makin' love as long as I am able
> Growin' corn and cotton too and when the day is over
> Ride the mule and cut the fool and love again all over.

Autumn has been a dizzying season. My mind has swung back and forth from the hellish to the heavenly effects of repetition. It was an odd pendulum swing. My mind clung for fleeting moments to a sense of wonder. It swung back and hovered endlessly over feelings of dullness. Enmeshed in daily tasks like shoveling manure or chain-sawing fallen branches, it was easy to get mired in the melancholy that attended repetitive tasks and the curse of Adam. Momentary redemption came from the transitory vision of beauty and simplicity in the soil and the flora and fauna it nurtured. It has been a cruel, wonderful, asymmetrical cycle, in which nature required work and then invited the heart to leap up.

Burial Mounds

I walked through the woods with a spade, the sharpest digging tool in my arsenal. I needed to find a burial site for a hen that expired overnight. It was easy to spot the deceased bird. *Rigor mortis* had set in quickly. The corpse lay in a position otherwise impossible for active chickens, with legs and neck outstretched. Eyelids, closed from the bottom upward, were stiff and dulled.

Outside the fence that encloses the barn lie several acres of woods, and it was there that I looked for a suitable burial plot. When I tried to heave the shovel with my shoulders or push it with my boots, it bounced off the ground. Granules of clay are tiny and therefore tightly packed. It would require a backhoe to dig beneath the frost line, or deep enough that scavengers could not detect a chicken corpse. There is also a network of roots, another challenge to the shovel. For softer earth, I looked for an uprooted tree, with loosened dirt around snapped roots. Or perhaps a fallen tree having been left to rot for a generation.

Burying a faithful hen honors the soil as well as the bird. Ideal soil has nitrogen, phosphorus, and other nutrients. It hosts enzymes and amino acids, both necessary for vegetation. The virtue of good dirt can best be defined by what herbicides destroy. The herbicide glyphosate, for example, blocks enzyme pathways, which otherwise make carbon compounds in food. Glyphosate also interrupts cellular communication and blocks the mycelial network. It kills bacteria and nutrients, allowing plants to be attacked by pests.

Glyphosate also reduces plant growth or causes death by impairing carbon metabolism and impeding the utilization of carbohydrates. Carbon is critical for healthy forage as well as for holding water. A buried chicken works in a tree's favor. A greater supply of carbon in turn helps the environment—it helps fertilize plants, which extract carbon from the atmosphere, thereby mitigating climate change.

By burying the fallen members of my flock, along with spreading wheelbarrows full of a decaying mixture of straw and poop, I returned to pre-industrial methods of fertilization, when fertilizer consisted chiefly of carbon-rich manure or compost. Modern farmers wage a war against carbon: chemical fertilizers contain no carbon; and deep tillage destroys soil networks while it releases soil carbon into the atmosphere.

The laying life of a hen is surprisingly short, only two to three years. They can survive a few years longer, but many farmers find it too costly to feed unproductive livestock. Peri names our hens—a challenge to the imagination as their number approached one hundred—which means that she would never agree to cull the flock. Our hens patiently wait for old age, never fearing that they will become soup or cacciatore. Since they are free range, however, they cannot always avoid predators. Raccoons and possums have killed a few for fun. I have discovered mangled, but uneaten, featherless corpses. Hawks and falcons are ever-present dangers. I have found chicken corpses in the fields, because plump, waddling chickens are usually too heavy for a predatory bird to hoist.

Whether from predator or organ failure, death on the farm is frequent, and my burial rites complemented Peri's efforts at baptism. I may be short on ceremony, but I like to honor those who bequeathed so many eggs to us with a grave deep enough to avoid scavengers.

Squawk Box

On the way to the barn my daily ruminations were interrupted by farm anxieties: has rain or wind encouraged a massive branch to fall on the barn; has a snake slithered among the birds; has a rooster plucked all the feathers from a feckless hen's back. Most feared of all is a predator's attack. Hawks circle at one hundred yards, and snakes sneak underneath the walls. I have seen several black snakes in the barn, ranging from foot-long youngsters to adult five-footers. So far, they have not appeared threatening to the chickens themselves—they rest quietly among the chickens like visitors from distant farms—but they devour eggs.

On entering the barn before daybreak, I began to rearrange straw to cover the ground and collect moisture and random droppings. I filled bins with chick crumble and layer feed. I marveled at the new wisdom I had acquired since abandoning Manhattan for a farm: I could observe the differences between chicken and guinea poop; I knew the protein levels of various 50-pound sacks of layer pellets; I knew the proper ratio of gas and oil to power a chain saw.

I also knew the habits of predators. Hawks, owls, falcons, raccoons, and possums have attacked our flock. Fortunately, the chickens find their way to the barn at dusk, and I lock them in overnight. Guineas, however, often prefer to spend their evenings perched on high branches, especially in the summer when the foliage is lush. The fate I dreaded most, the one that interrupted my daily walk to the barn most persistently, was to find the remains of a guinea.

Today I sensed that one of our guineas had been attacked overnight. The evidence of a predator attack built slowly. One small pile of white under-feathers, and larger purple feathers with white dots, signaled a tussle among sparring birds. Two piles was more ominous. Four piles signaled a nightmarish death struggle, probably instigated by an owl or a hawk. Mortality was confirmed by the morning's census count. There were five royal purple guineas and four—not five—African white. One of the latter was missing. After this attack, I found the carcass in a distant pasture, headless and mutilated. Sensing a struggle, our pack of Dobermans dashed from the house. Detecting the smell of the predator, they traced the frantic movements of the victim. They knew more about the overnight battle than I did.

So did the remaining guineas. The morning after the attack the guineas were silent. They knew they had lost a comrade. Instead of flocking to my morning treat of cracked corn, they walked together to another pasture. On the way they reassembled in a circle. Their chatter was quieter than usual. And instead of loudly squawking simultaneously they made sounds, almost sotto voce, sequentially. Perhaps they were rehearsing the battle or simply mourning. Slowly they moved on, further still, from the barn. Then, as usual, one or two perched on high branches and looked out for predators, communicating with the flock. The next evening, they wound their way, single file through the pasture, and entered the barn.

Holes

One bright and dewy morning I laid a shovel upon my shoulder, clutched a strong-jawed wire cutter, and trekked toward the creek. Chickens clucked from the barn, and in the distance the creek burbled over rock clusters. The hillside the creek has carved through has gotten steeper every year, as heavy downpours create rivulets that join to create floodwaters, which erode the clay and soil. The steeper a patch of land became, the more quickly the flooding carved into the top layers of earth, exposing rocks, animal skulls, and decaying tractor parts long since abandoned.

Dozens of yards of barbed wire that I intended to uproot and disassemble clutched rusted iron posts. A generation ago, the fence separated distinct parcels of land, but vines, bushes, and trees have since sprouted to create a sense of chaos without borders. I wanted to create a thinned expanse of woods with walks unhindered by natural or artificial obstructions. Fallen branches cluttered the route, and I trod carefully around aboveground roots and large rocks. But, with scattered leaves giving the illusion of level ground, one leg plunged into a hole the size of a watermelon. Undeterred, my other leg continued to lurch forward. A bolt of pain jolted my limbs as I landed on my wire cutters. My ankle would be useless for a while.

Our woods are pocked with holes. Snakes, chipmunks, squirrels, skunks, raccoons, groundhogs, mice—many animals burrow underground—seeking protection or setting traps. Some holes are shallow, some as deep as the rabbit hole in *Alice's Adventures in Wonderland.*

In addition to the myriad holes in the woods, uprooted trees gouged the earth, leaving open pits with rotted roots at their bases. All might overturn a small tractor, twist an ankle, or shatter a tibia or fibula. Nothing can interrupt my silent admiration for tufts of daffodils, or my observations of finely detailed rooster feathers, or my singing favorite songs as much as the consciousness of holes. I am often tempted to fill the tunnels, and I have been known to cart wheelbarrows full of clay from hole to hole to smooth out the earth. After all, one moment of absentminded dreaming, or a veneer of fallen leaves, is all that stands between me and injury. But it takes only one annual cycle to realize that I've undertaken yet another Sisyphean task, for the snakes and mice return to dig new holes if they cannot find the old ones. It is difficult to simply let nature be. The only practical alternative is eternal vigilance.

Thoreau remarked that he built his house upon a hole. "I dug my cellar in the side of a hill sloping to the south, where a woodchuck had formerly dug his burrow, down through sumach and blackberry roots, and the lowest stain of vegetation. . . ." A typical passage in *Walden,* in which the literal and mundane morph easily into the philosophical and sublime. The passage hints at a sort of biblical wisdom in the notion of a house built upon nothing. Thoreau nods at his atavistic drive and his delight in animal spirits by building his house upon the lodgings of a woodchuck. The notion of original sin floats over the passage's phrase "lowest stain." But all of this philosophical musing is built upon literally nothing—the image of a hole in the ground.

I struggled to my feet, and leaning my wire cutter against a tree, hobbled toward the house, winding around ruptures in the earth. My good leg soon grew weary from dragging the injured one uphill. And when I finally reached level ground, I tripped into another hole, this one a shallow bowl. Chickens and guineas had scratched into the earth and burrowed into pits to cover their feathers with clouds of dirt. Dust baths reduce their load of parasites and bacteria. In the pounding heat of summer, these baths also cool fowl body temperature, while offering a few moments of rest between long stretches of scratching for insects. I rested a moment myself, before limping onward.

Olfactory Sensations

One spring morning I opened the porch door into a soupy blue-gray mist that enveloped the trees and hovered over the bushes. Gibbs, who usually dashed out the door and led the way to the barn, stopped mid-lurch and turned to me with a confused look. The fog even obscured my boots, and I walked with a halting pace. The still air muffled the usual sounds of leaves rustling and birds chirping. I could measure every yard of the walk to the woods only by smell. First, sweet camellia blossoms perfumed the air. Then thickly massed azaleas emitted a woozy odor, less sweet but just as potent. I could not distinguish the twined smells emitted by lilies, daffodils, roses, and hyacinths, but they grew stronger as I walked toward the barn.

Fumes from chicken poop punched through the air as I crossed the pasture. Opening the barn door at dawn always shocked the olfactory system. A breath of sweet morning air was followed by a slap of ammonia from the condensed and stagnant poop dripping from ledges and littered in the straw.

Gibbs was busy following the footsteps of night visitors, his nose tracing long curves on the ground. He always made me aware of the array of odors I could not detect. His nose looks like a rubber electrical outlet, not firmly attached on either side. Dogs have exponentially more nasal and complementary brain cells than humans. Gibbs, nose to the ground, seemed to follow invisible trails of deer, snakes, groundhogs, and other critters. The exquisite delicacy of this animal sense does not result in a gag reaction to animal droppings. My first dog, then the second and third, happily perused piles of horse droppings the size of a cantaloupe. They are contented coprophagiacs, gobbling down excrement without a trace of disgust.

I have scoured *Walden* for insight into the sense of smell. Thoreau wandered his woods and fields with heightened sense impressions and an insistence on the importance of the body. In the burgeoning industrial age of railroads, he saw his neighbors mired with domestic duties and caught in a spiral of mind-numbing, commercial activities, and attempted to make them aware of their rootedness in the earth. At the beginning of *Walden*'s fifth chapter, "Solitude," he treated us to the contemplation of all our senses joining forces: "This is a delicious evening, when the whole body is one sense, and imbibes delight through every pore." An amazing sentence, each clause a variation on the theme of synesthesia.

Of all the senses, the least present in Thoreau's woods was the sense of smell. I can recall only one instance in *Walden* in which Thoreau mentioned his sense of smell: when the lingering odor of cigar or pipe smoke signaled to him that a traveler had passed his cabin. It was not a sensation from nature, and it did not engender a sense of delight. Rather, it was simply a clue that led him to detect the recent presence of a visitor.

Just a few wisps of fog remained as I left the barn to run the dog in the woods. There I detected a different variety of smoke from four hundred paces, a whiff of burning carbon. Soon, grey tufts emitted from burned leaves and branches choked my lungs. Smoke had spiraled from a neighbor's property as the wind shifted. Fire threatened to dance along the hills. But soon a different odor reached my nose, flames sputtering on damp leaves. Thoreau didn't make much use of odors, but that morning I had navigated my way, and sensed danger, by my olfactory sensations.

Habit

When I returned from the barn at dusk, coated with clay dust and sweat, Peri greeted me in the back porch with a laundry basket. Struggling to pull off my boots, she asked what chores I could now scratch off my list. I stood silent for a few moments, and Peri must have thought I was journeying ever closer to dementia. I scarcely remembered what I had accomplished over the previous ten hours.

Over the past few months, I walked to the barn every sunrise to release the chickens from their stall and give them their daily treat of cracked corn. I bush-hogged several pastures weekly. I planted buckwheat and clover annually. All this activity had become hardwired in my brain and sinews. It had become habit. A good habit has the virtue of preserving energy and saving time. Without it, we would have to figure out how to schedule every task from the moment we awaken. We are all "mere bundles of habit," as William James taught us over a century ago.

James was a subtle enough thinker to realize both the blessings and the curse of habit. On the one hand, habit enables us to handle tasks more easily over time; it sets the brain free to calculate, imagine, and invent. This is the American pragmatist version of the human mental feature that results from repetition. It began with Franklin, for whom it was even more valuable—it underwrote the practice of the virtues. On the other hand, habit dulls the mind. It restricts our physical, intellectual, and moral potential. According to James, I had been making "very small use of [my] possible consciousness and of [my] soul's resources in general."

The dark side of habit was at the heart of Walker Percy's vision. Habit, for Percy, was the gravitational pull toward mental and moral emptiness. In *The Moviegoer*, habit was the mediocrity of the everyday, which prevents us from searching, from escaping despair and meaninglessness. The danger of habit for Percy was existential and personal. For Twain it was social and moral. In *Pudd'nhead Wilson*, habit underwrote not virtue but prejudice—the deep racial prejudice that radiated throughout Twain's post-bellum America. It was a burden that prevented people from changing their fundamental nature. It was a curse that rivaled original sin.

As I peeled off my frayed dungarees before Peri, I cleaved to the darker view of habit. I yearned for a sense of accomplishment. If I performed my daily chores, I should at least have a feeling of closure, of happiness even. Eggs were collected, lawns manicured, and fallen branches picked up that day. But the very notion of habit told my dulled brain that these tasks must be repeated. Any sense of virtuous action was like a wisp of fog—unsubstantial and evanescent. Satisfaction guaranteed to last at most until nightfall. My life on the farm is lived in the present perfect tense: my actions are in the past, but not yet complete.

Poop

On one still summer morning, releasing the chickens from the barn, I was assaulted by a putrid olfactory sensation. The chickens must have consumed a bad batch of insects the previous day, and the barn was dripping with liquified poop. My disgust response closed my esophagus, slowed my breathing, and pushed my body backwards.

Chickens have no bowel control, and they have no desire to wait until break of day to release their waste. As a result, overnight they plaster roosts and every surface of the barn with poop. I thought I had become accustomed to the odor. I had learned to soften it with a layer of straw or sand on the barn floor. But that morning the odor gave me a concussion.

Struggling to regain consciousness, I wondered how anyone could have discovered a use for animal droppings. Perhaps that's why ancient folk apotheosized the farmer who discovered manure. According to the Romans, fields once languished for lack of fertilizer. No one had thought of transferring animal excrement to tilled fields until an obscure farmer made this world-shattering discovery. This quantum leap in human productivity was noted by no less than Augustine in his *The City of God*: "Stercutus, being a most skillful husbandman, discovered that the fields could be fertilized by the dung of animals, which is called *stercus* from his name." Latin is rich with words whose etymologies derive from this demigod. According to Isidore of Seville's *Etymologies*, "Stercutus first brought the technique of dunging (*stercorare*) fields to Italy. . . . He invented many agricultural tools, and was the first to enrich fields."

Dung, manure, poop, shit—English has many words for excrement, and the concept has acquired a multitude of meanings. Aside from bodily waste, it can connote just plain stuff ("move this shit out of the house"), desultory or inflammatory words ("bullshit"), a person's mental facility ("get your shit together"), extreme fear ("scared shitless"), trouble ("you're in deep shit"), and expressions of disrespect or surprise ("eat shit" or "holy shit!").

Our word "shit" began with the Old English *shite* (defecation), *shitte* (diarrhea), and *beshitan* (to cover with excrement). Linguistic descendants from the Old English were used in Chaucer's *Canterbury Tales*. Shit has been associated with Ben Jonson's anal compulsive hoarding of money on the one hand and with Jonathan Swift's horror of female sexuality on the other. My favorite couplet ends Swift's poem "Cassinus and Peter: A Tragical Elegy": "Nor wonder how I lost my Wits; Oh! *Cælia, Cælia, Cælia* sh---."

One place I did not expect to hear much about waste products was in *Walden*. Thoreau's tendency was to link the spirit with the body, or intelligence with instinct—but not to focus on the mundane. "I have been thrilled to think that I owed a mental perception to the commonly gross sense of taste," he wrote in "Higher Laws." His interest was to redeem the body and base instincts. But in a wonderful passage in "Spring" he lavished attention upon thawing sand that flows down banks created by the railroad. "The sand begins to flow down the slopes like lava," creating innumerable little streams that resemble "bowels, and excrements of all kinds." He delighted in the many heaps of fertile nature's decay, which he called "excrementitious."

I derived no ecological or historical delight from excrement. At best, it offers clues to animal behavior, for it is possible to identify animals from their droppings. There are the small oval deer droppings and the cylindrical guinea droppings. The color scheme of the oddly shaped blobs of chicken droppings, half white and half brown, resemble old American crockery. There are amorphous piles of dog poop, and the extremely large tootsie roll segments that accumulate in the mounds of horse manure.

It is more difficult to find droppings of raccoons, foxes, snakes, and skunks. Many animals do not want to leave a physical or odoriferous trace. When I find these unusual droppings, I can identify predators. My Doberman does not rely on visual clues. Her nose scours the ground for scatological evidence of animals that have long since absconded.

I gave the barn stall time to air before re-entering. For the next twenty minutes I scooped the scattered excrement into a five-gallon bucket with a trowel and a barn rake. Then I lugged the bucket behind the fence to the manure pile at the end of a back pasture. The pile had grown from a plateau to a pyramid in a couple of months. A miasma of poop hovered over the pile but remained behind the fence. After the pile ages I will follow Stercutus's advice and spread the poop-straw mixture on Peri's garden. The droppings are very high in nitrogen, potassium, and phosphorus, which makes chicken manure good for vegetables. Horse manure, which I collect behind Oliver's barn, is better for acid-loving plants, such as blueberries, azaleas, mountain laurel, and rhododendrons. The good farmer really knows his, well, manure.

Faith in Animal Nature

Near daybreak, I walked our two Dobermans around the perimeter of the property for their morning constitutional. The puppy, Danni, was zestful. She dashed about, nipping at her older sibling's paws and prodding him to play. Gibbs refused to be goaded and trotted steadily forward. But suddenly they raced away together, stopping in the middle of the field. When I caught up with them, I pulled them away from a mangled body. There lay one of our Silver Laced Wyandottes, her skull cracked open. A nocturnal predator, presumably an owl, had feasted on her brains. The carcass seemed to ignite blood lust in the dogs. Their noses prodded the blood-stained feathers as they snarled at the midnight murderer. As for me, my stomach churned. Farm life had not yet inoculated me against my revulsion at the bloodletting in the food chain. Animals instinctively hunt for protein, but it takes time to accustom oneself to the natural order of things.

I have read arguments in the philosophical debate about empathy—whether it is a virtue, as it is for Adam Smith and Jane Austen, whether it is helpful, whether it is rational, whether it acts in accord with justice, whether it responds more favorably to certain individuals, whether it violates equity with prejudice against distant groups of people. I'm fervently on the pro-empathy side of the argument, except on the farm. On the farm, empathy can be a burden. It has made me feel the pain of the beheaded bird and the swallowed frog. It has not helped steel my nerves. Rather, it has worked against me as I try to keep my emotional distance from the slaughter.

But along with impersonal brutality, a counterforce acts in nature, one that crosses species. Last winter we ordered three varieties of pullets from a hatchery. For several weeks, we nurtured seventeen chicks in the laundry room, where they resided in a large bin with a heat lamp clamped on a drawer overhead. The chicks seemed to double in size every six hours. It was like watching a baby go to college a couple of weeks after you've changed the last diaper. After about a month they grew to such an extent that they could no longer scurry about in their tub. So, when a March cold front blew north, I transferred them to a coop outside the barn.

Most of the time, chickens walk, eat, and sleep with their own kind. We rarely see a Black Copper Maran in the midst of heritage Barred Rock chickens. African White and Royal Purple guinea fowl move together as a pack, but each color forms a distinct sub-group. But when we introduced the pullets to the pasture, the guineas took it upon themselves to guard the coop. Coops are hazardous for chickens. Without the lamp overhead, even huddling may not offer them enough warmth. Plus, hungry carnivores can dig under coops and gorge themselves. The guineas were ready to fend off any attack if a snake or predatory bird should approach.

Gibbs also showed remarkable paternalism. At first, he chased chickens and guineas for sport. Now he plods amongst them like an unruffled nanny. Gibbs' younger companion, Danni, lurched at everything on two legs when she arrived at Hyacinth Farm. When we brought her out to the pasture for the first time, her legs flew in every direction as she flashed toward any fowl that moved. But at race car speeds, with sudden lurches and stops, Gibbs put himself between Danni and the chickens' necks. His barks seemed designed to mentor the newcomer in the ways of the farm. And soon, Danni also walked calmly amongst the flock.

Last week a fire destroyed our friends' cabin in the woods. They reached out to us not for food, clothing, or shelter but for a home for their chickens. So far, they have been able to catch only one white Leghorn. Chickens don't appreciate newcomers inserted into the established hierarchies of their flock. In her first days with us, the refugee hen often wandered into the woods or roosted alone on a bench far from the clucking crowd. But one rooster, a Black Maran, began protecting her. Now he wanders off with her and stands by her until she returns to the flock. Peri has named him Windsor, and we watch this prince from our window—easy to spot as his majestic bronze, black, and orange feathers stand out against the hen's pure white.

As Peri and I herded our birds into the barn two weeks after the Leghorn's arrival, a row of adolescent guineas planted themselves on a maple branch behind the fence. For them, it must have seemed like the wilderness. They squawked in response to our pleas to come in. The noise must have alerted predators. The next morning all but one of them had vanished, likely carried off by hawks or owls. The survivor lay sprawled on the ground, one leg dangling by a thin stretch of skin. Peri swaddled the bird and carried it back to the house cradled in her arms. Every evening for two weeks, I held his wings close to his wriggling body as Peri injected him with an antibiotic. She then nestled a dropper into his mouth and delivered medicine for pain and inflammation. Finally, I spread Neosporin on the back of the severed tendons behind the knee and bandaged the wound.

The injured guinea—Peri named him Browning—survived, but the ripped tendons never healed. The leg curled toward his body, and he hopped for short distances, trying to keep his balance. We kept him caged for several weeks as other birds pecked or shunned him. After we released him, seeing if he could feed himself, he learned how to avoid the bullies. Soon he could hop all day, even climb steps, without falling.

One day I found him balanced, motionless, near a colleague. On closer inspection, he was standing guard over a female warming a nest of eggs. They remained in the brooding and protector positions for six weeks, until twenty keets hatched. Over the following weeks, Browning hopped beside the little ones as they moseyed in the pasture in front of the barn. Once a pariah, he was now the father figure for the next generation. Browning's perseverance and commitment to the community that had shunned him buttressed my faith in animal nature.

Snakes

Dave had been burrowing under the house for most of the morning, insulating the crawl space to create a vapor barrier. We wanted to keep humidity, frigid air, and critters from entering the house at ground level. At noon he wriggled out of the cavern cradling one such creature, a *Pantherophis alleghaniensis*, or black rat snake. I recoiled at the sight of a flickering tongue and four feet of shiny leathery skin coiled on Dave's arm. He calmly stroked the snake, which remained motionless, and offered the sleek blackness to me to caress. I politely declined.

Locals know which species are poisonous. This one obviously was not. Dave told me that black snakes also keep down the mouse population and kill copperheads. We walked to the woods and dropped it off gently. I suspect it slithered down toward the creek.

Later that afternoon, Dave plunged out of the crawl space, yelling for mothballs. After he calmed down, he told me that snakes are repelled by the chemical in mothballs; he wanted to spread them around the baby copperhead with which he had come face-to-face. Copperheads are poisonous, and baby copperheads more so, as they tend to eject all their poison with the first injection (adults hold a bit back for the second and third bites).

Copperheads are more camouflaged than black snakes, as their mottled brown scales blend in with fallen leaves and branches. I have since encountered a few in my pasture-clearing escapades. Like humans, they sometimes put pleasure above survival. I have seen a couple extended on our driveway, absorbing the heat, oblivious to crushing wheels or stick-wielding youth. Mainly, however, they lie hidden in holes or under piles of branches, precisely the locations where our Gibbs and Danni like to stick their snouts. I found Gibbs one day acting sluggish, his tail underneath his body, looking embarrassed. We found a puncture wound on his cheek and called the vet. Peri spent the next few hours holding an intravenous bag over our wounded warrior.

The copperhead's scientific name, *Agkistrodon controtrix*, means hooked-tooth twister. They are particularly active, notes David George Haskell in *The Forest Unseen*, on muggy summer evenings. Their favorite snack is cicadas, and you can find snakes on the prowl when the insects crawl up from their underground larval burrows. Every county in North Carolina has copperheads, and farmers and their children know their habits, their prey, and their dens.

Farmers walk in rubber boots in fields with grasses of even modest height lest they unwittingly rouse and threaten a snake.

The battle between farmers and snakes has a storied history in America. The Pilgrim John Winthrop, Governor of Massachusetts Bay Colony, wrote in his diary that when a snake had entered a church an elder "trod upon the head of it." He sermonized that the serpent was the devil and that the faithful "overcame him and crushed his head."

The battle went the other way in de Crèvecoeur's *Letters from an American Farmer*. De Crèvecoeur moralized the farmer, not the snake. At the time of the Revolution, he wrote that the farmer personified the freedom and independence of the new American. Snakes were mortal threats, not Satan. In his tenth letter, he told of a farmer whose boots had protected him from a venomous strike. Unfortunately, however, the snake's fangs lodged in the boot leather. When the farmer pulled his boots off, the detached fang scratched his leg, which resulted in a mysterious swelling and a strange sickness in his stomach. Death quickly followed. All of this is told as a sort of medical detective story—after the deaths of others who tried on the farmer's boots, the doctor ultimately discovered the fangs.

Crèvecoeur's two distinct ways of describing snakes presaged the realist and romantic strains in American literature. First, he sought to describe the dimensions, facility, poisonous sacks, and colors of snakes. He separated the poisonous from the harmless species. He offered medical details about the mortality of snake bites. Two centuries later, many local farmers are just as practical and careful about snakes. They know how to identify the various species or avoid the rocks and wood piles in which they rest. I've also learned from them that guinea fowl are useful in keeping the snake population under control. When a snake intrudes upon their feeding grounds, the birds quickly surround it, run in a circle, and ultimately dive in for the kill.

The romantic prose of Crèvecoeur offers a jarring contrast to the realist descriptions. The tale of the epic battle of the snakes is the most memorable passage in his *Letters from an American Farmer*. It has the power of the famous scene in the *Aeneid* in which snakes emerged from the sea to strangle Laocoon and his sons. One day as the narrator walked through his fields, he heard a rustling but could see nothing. Suddenly

> to my astonishment, I beheld two snakes of considerable length, the one pursuing the other with great celerity through a hemp-stubble field . . . They soon met, and, in the fury of their first encounter, appeared in an instant firmly twisted together; and while their united tails beat the ground, they mutually tried, with open jaws to lacerate each other.

An epic battle ensued—with fiery eyes, twisting sinews, and muscular writhing—until one snake forcibly drowned the other and then unceremoniously returned to shore and disappeared. The narration is driven by powerful emotions. The snakes radiated courage and fury. The narrator was astonished and filled with dread and admiration for their uncommon beauty.

It is difficult not to harbor a sense of dread toward snakes, or a sense of wonder at their beauty. Cultural associations also burden many of us, as D.H. Lawrence depicts in his poem "Snake." In the poem, "on a hot, hot day," a snake reaches a water trough ahead of the poet with his pitcher. As he waited his turn, Lawrence's effort to simply observe the snake failed. Visions intruded. His education taught him to see the Biblical snake as well as the Greek mythological Typhon upon which Zeus hurled Mount Etna, but not the thirsty creature before him. His culturally imbibed dread, and perhaps his cowardice, impelled him to throw a log at the retreating snake. He was instantly ashamed of his pettiness but still could not shed the romantic layers of meaning.

Snakes continually surprised folks in the early American landscape. William Bartram trekked through the Carolinas and other southern colonies around the time of the Revolution to document plant species for science and profit. He narrated two snake encounters in his *Travels*. While looking for plants in the swamps of east Florida, "my father bid me observe the rattlesnake before and just at my feet." Bartram saw "the monster formed in a high spiral coil, not half his length from my feet."

Battling resentment toward his father for his keener sense of observation, he killed the snake with a branch. Later, Seminoles entreated Bartram to remove a large snake from their camp. The botanist and great collector of animals was reluctant but was forced to concede to his hosts' wishes.

> I took out my knife, severed his [the great rattlesnake's] head from his body, then turning about, the Indians complimented me with every demonstration of satisfaction and approbation for my heroism, and friendship for them. I carried off the head of the serpent bleeding in my hand as a trophy of victory; and taking out the mortal fangs, deposited them carefully amongst my collections.

Wonder and the mundane coexisted in Bartram's world. He easily modulated from a prayer to the Creator of nature's grandeur to a discussion of land as real estate. The multitude of species of flora and fauna was proof of God's glory and cause of the vast inventory of a merchant's shelves. In the case of snakes, a description of one of his epic battles was followed abruptly by a catalogue. Besides rattlers, there are the less monstrous moccasins, vipers, green snakes, chicken snakes, bull snakes, ribbands, horn snakes, and others. This catalogue seems mundane, following as it does the horrors and resentments of the close encounters. On the one hand, the lavishly described colors, the measurements, and observations of flora created finely drawn realistic descriptions. On the other, the self-consciousness and swirl of heightened emotions created a world of gothic romance.

After Dave left for the evening, I took Gibbs for a walk in the woods. Curving around a tuft of trees, we both spotted a giant black snake extended in the dying sunlight. Luxuriant, his blackness radiated an iridescent green sheen. I stiffened, and quietly urged the hapless Doberman to veer from the resting giant, who seemed unperturbed by our presence. A feeling of sublime beauty, grace, and power washed over me as I measured the snake's girth and calibrated its sprawling length to be about six feet. After a few moments, I felt my heart beat again, and the dog and I made our way to the woods.

Swerve

The cacophony of clucking and crowing softened as the sun sank into the branches of distant trees. Chickens returned to the barn from pastures and woods near and far and tranquilly pecked for a final snack before bedtime. As I approached the nesting boxes to collect eggs, dozens of birds dashed toward me, eager for corn kernels. Guinea fowl bobbled and squawked their way toward me, too. A few flapped their wings, flying and running at the same time to overtake their peers.

When I approached Oliver grazing in another pasture, he lifted his head, backed out of a tuft of daffodils, and trotted towards me in a parabolic curve, swerving toward me in the final few gallops. When Danni followed me into the horse pasture, she dashed straight toward a distant squirrel but came at it finally with a curving swoop. She never reached it and did not see it scamper up a tree. When I called her, she pretended to disobey, running at a 30-degree angle away from me. But then she swerved in an outflanking maneuver. She playfully attacked in a gentle swerve, swooping, in Hopkins's lovely phrase, "as a skate's heel sweeps smooth on a bow-bend."*

I now divide animals on the farm into two camps. Chickens and guineas sprint toward me in a straight

*From Hopkins's poem "The Windhover"

line. Danni and Oliver dash in curves. The first theorist of linear and curving lines was the Roman poet Lucretius. His philosophical poem *On the Nature of Things* was not based on observation of animals but on theories of things unseen. He hypothesized that atoms hurtled through space with a regular, downward linear motion. In order to explain free will, he wrote that one atom diverted from its natural course, swerved, and collided with another atom. The Lucretian swerve was the moment when stability in the universe changed. This swerve, or *clinamen* in Lucretius's Latin, was a violation of Newton's first law of motion, the law that a body in motion stays in motion with the same speed and in the same direction unless acted upon by an unbalanced force. Nothing could account for the sudden change in the motion of atoms in Lucretius's universe except free will.

Jonathan Swift satirized the Lucretian swerve. He defined *clinamen* in *A Tale of a Tub* as an inclination, a bias, or an unproven argument. Joyce turned this moment in Lucretian philosophy into a lovely description of a river in the opening of *Finnegan's Wake*: "riverrun, past Eve and Adam's [say this aloud, as *even atoms*], from swerve of shore to bend of bay. . . ."

I noticed how the swerve in the horse pasture differed from the dash among the chickens that evening. Danni loved to play by pretending to dash at, and then flank, the horse. Oliver was in his mid-thirties, a centenarian in human terms, but he reared and galloped toward the dog with the energy of a colt. Each ran in curves, trying to outflank the other. I had a bout of vertigo trying to follow their dance. I returned to the barn to close up the nesting boxes for the evening. A couple of roosters had not run out of testosterone and were still pursuing hens. The adolescent male initiated a direct assault. When one hen evaded his onslaught, he pivoted toward another. A farm with young roosters is a scene of constant sexual harassment. Once they mount, it is not unusual for them to rip neck and back feathers off their mate.

The mature rooster, on the other hand, was a subtle seducer. He danced a jig, circling the hen, who mirrored his steps in reverse, Ginger Rogers to his Fred Astaire. Then he gently mounted, left the hen unruffled, and departed.

I had observed the contrast between young and mature dancers once before in humans. When I lived in Budapest, a friend took me to a traditional Hungarian dance. The ballroom was crowded with couples in peasant costumes, and the band played village tunes *prestissimo*. One young man twirled so swiftly he barely touched the floor. Engrossed with his pyrotechnic moves, he lost sight of his partner. Meanwhile, across the stage, an older couple wound slowly around each other. Their arms guided and caressed, their eyes locked. The pair's movement was graceful, without an ounce of self-consciousness. I longed to be an older man.

So, I came to a complex understanding of animal geometry on the farm. Chickens approaching me for a treat waddle, trot, or dash in straight lines. Immature but sexually active roosters sprint directly at their prey. Mature roosters attract their harem with a mating dance that arabesques around the female. Danni and Oliver playfully, or stealthily, swerve to outflank their opponent.

As an amateur farm philosopher, I have not yet had the leisure to speculate on atoms and free will. I suspect that Lucretius never got dirt under his fingernails and had only a literary view of nature. For me, swerve changed the nature of the universe by adding mature courtship and play.

*Nature Red in Tooth and Claw**

Walking toward the barn during a typical morning mission of watering and feeding, I saw evidence to support the unsentimental, instinctual pursuit of breakfast in nature. I spotted a significant number of ruffled lavender feathers, and assumed I had lost one of the chickens. We have Black Copper Marans, heritage Barred Rocks, and lavenders. The latter are particularly plump; their attempts to run, impeded by the undulating mass of their rear ends, is hilarious. They are also the most aggressive of the three breeds, and the roosters are like gang members continuously trying to prove their dominance. So, I was not surprised to find the remains of a fight. I searched around the pasture, and when I could not find the injured bird, I entered the barn. There lay the prostrate, formerly proud, rooster. The straw had absorbed a pint of blood, which had oozed out of its mangled neck and fleshless skull. A predator had barely eaten any of its prize. A raccoon, or perhaps a fox, had killed for fun.

There's a lot of local lore in the genre of nature's struggle for survival. One neighbor has told me about a coyote carrying off her chickens, as they huddled in

*From Alfred Lord Tennyson's poem *In Memoriam*

a cage, for a family meal. Another saw an owl land on a branch near a sleeping guinea fowl, inch closer, nudge it off the branch, swoop down, and clutch it in razor sharp claws. I recently had followed white polka dotted black feathers through a pasture until I spotted a guinea carcass missing a liver and other sumptuous organs. And, horrified, I once spotted blood-spattered feeders next to the barn, evidence of a hawk carrying off two African white guineas.

Tennyson posed a philosophical question in 1850, nine years before Darwin published *On the Origin of the Species*. How can you logically move from the violent laws of nature to Creation's final law of love?

I don't think theologians are much troubled by the question any longer. Biologists, neuroscientists, psychologists, anthropologists, and philosophers of consciousness, however, do try within their professional paradigms to discover what *Homo sapiens* inherited from our prehuman ancestors. But violence, in Tennyson's sense of "nature red in tooth and claw," is not an inherited characteristic. The carnivore on the savannah (or the hawk or raccoon on the farm) is not exactly violent. It is driven by instinct and hunger to devour protein. I keep an eye on hawks and take measures to keep raccoons from entering the barn because they are hungry, not because these creatures are mean-spirited. Tennyson should rather have asked how our species went from killing for food to murder for profit or vengeance. Violence, anger, and murder are distinctly human attributes.

Memento Mori

On a chilly autumn morning, I meandered through the woods, inspecting the damage an overnight thunderstorm had caused. Branches littered the path. A pine had cracked mid-trunk. The fallen half was still attached to the base by a few bark strands, creating a right triangle. Rivulets of water had carved trenches that descended to the creek.

But among the detritus lay evidence of a generative life force. A guinea egg nestled in a nest of oak leaves; a host of chicken of the woods mushrooms burst out of a maple trunk like bright orange blossoms; a small family of deer nibbled green tips of underbrush.

My tour of the storm damage ended at the barn. As I looked for evidence of flooding, I stumbled upon a rooster lying stiffly on his side. He rested on a pile of feathers, his back pierced and his eyelids rolling up to their final close. The snuffing out of élan and beauty—the stunning assembly of bronze, orange, and black feathers—knocked the breath out of me.

I could not know for certain how this rooster died. I suspected my Dobermans. The two romped innocently when alone; together, they morphed into a predatory pack. Once I left them alone only for a moment, and when I returned, I found four dead fowl scattered among three pastures. There were no feathers or other clues on the murderers, nor were the hounds huddled around their prey. But my sharp-toothed dogs are more likely than a bevy of hawks or a daytime raccoon to have slain the flock of chickens.

I grabbed the rooster's legs and paced toward my animal burial plot to the rhythm of Mozart's *Requiem*. My mood bounced back and forth between elation and desperation, joy and depression, firm resolve and helplessness. I rested comfortably in one emotional extreme before jolting toward the other. Life on the farm accommodated my manic spirit. Nothing dampened my happiness upon discovering a newly laid egg or the burst of an orange blossom. And then nothing relieved the burden of mortal thoughts upon discovering a slaughtered animal. As Shakespeare said, "Two loves I have, of comfort and despair." I struggled to find an emotional middle ground, something to relieve the toll of swinging between optimism and despair. I had been a disciple of the Aristotelian mean, which calibrates where virtue lies. Courage, for example, lies between recklessness and cowardice. But on the farm, what lay between emotional highs and lows was mediocrity and boredom.

The image of the rooster's mangled body was seared into my brain that day. His last breath became a haunting memory. The rational mind can categorize death. It does not minimize horror, but it places it in the context of a wonderful cycle of nature. And a long line of thinkers has conditioned us to prepare for death. Socrates in the *Phaedo,* and his Stoic disciples Seneca and Epictetus, counseled us to dismiss the power of death. But the chicken's slaughter and thoughts of death hovered over me well into the evening like thick ash after a volcanic eruption. The idea of a Christian heaven did not offer any consolation, nor did the notion of a pagan spring. My only nourishment was despair, what the poet Gerard Manley Hopkins called carrion comfort.

Hopkins worked his way through his dark night of the soul, but there are long periods during which I cannot. Loss was often my dominant feeling on the farm. Saint John Chrysostom taunted the once powerful deity, "O Death, where is thy sting?" I respond that the sting of death is forever on the land.

As I dwelt upon mortality, my thoughts drifted and spiraled. My ruminations followed the path of a florid style of writing, with cascading dependent clauses that wind their way toward a period. Grammatical pedants like me label this style hypotactic. At the other end of the spectrum is the paratactic style, curt and bare of ornament, often devoid of adjectives and adverbs. Such sentences consist only of the necessary parts of speech.

The first style tends to be ornate or heavily moral. The most judgmental of poets, Dante and Milton, come to mind, but in each case the author is everywhere apparent. Annie Dillard called our attention to the paradox in *Living by Fiction.* She pointed out how this sort of prose can "penetrate and dazzle." It calls attention to itself, "waving its arms as it were, while performing metaphysics behind its back." It is a profligate and "spendthrift" style that is

> dense in objects which pester the senses. It hauls in visual imagery of every sort; it strews metaphors about, and bald similes, and allusions to every realm. It does not shy from adjectives, nor even from adverbs. It traffics in parallel structures

and repetitions; it indulges in assonance and alliteration.

The paratactic style, by contrast, is abrupt and direct; it invites the reader to inspect the information it offers rather than the writer who offers it. It tends to be more appropriate for observation than meditation.

The florid hypotactic style often correlates with the intensely inward mind. It frequently accompanies morose moods and bouts of depression. Nowhere is this more apparent than in the journals of Lewis and Clark. Lewis's entries were often arabesque, with phrases as intricate as the brocade on a gentleman's cuff. They tended to ramble and ponder. He ruminated, abandoning observation and leaving nature behind. Over time, his thoughts trended toward darkness. In fact, Lewis committed suicide a few years after the famous trek.

Clark, on the other hand, tended to write simple sentences—not simple-minded, but crisp and appropriate for journals jam-packed with fresh observations. It is often Clark who jotted down naturalist observations and measurements. Lewis was more likely to record customs, sentiments, and anxieties:

> Our vessels consisted of six small canoes, and two large perogues. This little fleet altho' not quite rispectable as those of Columbus or Capt. Cook, were still viewed by us with as much pleasure as those deservedly famed adventurers ever beheld theirs; and I dare say with quite as much anxiety for their safety and preservation. We were now about to penetrate a country at least two thou-

> sand miles in width, on which the foot of civillized man had never trodden; the good or evil it had in store for us was for experiment yet to determine, and these little vessells contained every article by which we were to expect to subsist or defend ourselves. However as this the state of mind in which we are, generally gives the colouring to events, when the immagination is suffered to wander into futurity, the picture which now presented itself to me was a most pleasing one . . .

American literature after Lewis and Clark could be divided into two camps: the sinuous and florid style, the long clauses, the description of consciousness, and the descent into morose musings of Lewis on the one hand; and on the other, Clark's terse style that focused on observation, surfaces, and facts. Faulkner and Hemingway define the outer limits of the hypo- and paratactic styles. Thomas Pynchon, the notorious post-modernist novelist, put this pair of styles at the thematic center of *Mason & Dixon*. This vast sprawling novel is about a line of demarcation drawn on a map and on a country by two astronomers. Each hero corresponds, in mental activity and style, to the latter pair of explorers: Mason is as self-conscious, depressive, and imaginative as Lewis, while Dixon is as unreflective, optimistic, and limited to the world of observation and measurement as Clark. The binary oppositions they defined appeared in the colonies whose boundaries they surveyed and the kinds of Americans they encountered.

Mason and Dixon divided the world of the mind between them as surely as they separated Maryland from Pennsylvania. The division reflected their differing world views. I could easily project their map onto the farm, where one guinea egg nestled in leaves lay across the border from the mangled rooster.

Pynchon Footnote

Here is a partial listing of thematic pairs in *Mason & Dixon*:

Lewis	Clark
Maryland	Pennsylvania
song	calculus
mopish	cheerful
self-conscious	heedless
doubt	reason
probability	certainty
may	must
muse	observe
ingenious	traditional
imagination	vision
reverse squint	telescope
desire	observation
poetry	measurement
myth	astronomy
curve	straight line
Holy Ghost	George III
dithyramb	American hymn
rapture	law
leisure	productivity
subjunctive	declarative

The Barking Dogs Were Silent

Dogs have a checkered history in the rural South. Their various species play vital roles in outdoor work crews. Hounds attend hunters. Farmers let loose the dogs of war among herds of livestock to fend off coyotes and other predators. Small landholders keep rottweilers and pit bull terriers to warn potential burglars. Frequently, however, experiments with canine protection services go awry. A dog trained to be vigilant, even violent, might become a bit too aggressive with a child or unruly with the master. Impatience and frustration often lead to dog abandonment. The many animal shelters and rescue operations are a testament to the hordes of dogs left to fend for themselves on the backroads and in the woods. The vast majority of dogs in county shelters are pit bulls, but there are rescues that specialize in Dobermans, greyhounds, border collies, and several other varieties.

It is risky to purchase a dog from an animal rescue organization. Many of these dogs are psychologically damaged from battered early lives. Peri and I have heard tales of dogs that were tortured with curling irons, tethered under the North Carolina summer sun for weeks on end, or used for target practice. At the very least, such animals will exhibit signs of depression and remain wary of new owners for months.

Nevertheless, we decided to make a better life for one of these dogs while at the same time adding vitality to the farm. Our first rescue was a Doberman, a species not necessarily known for herding chickens but notorious for its intelligence. We drove ten hours south to the Georgia-Florida border to get this new family addition, and he seemed to take to us immediately, leaping into our car and waiting patiently for 600 miles. Gibbs had been abandoned at least twice in his four years, once left in a field for months when his owner traveled over a thousand miles to another state. For several weeks after our first Memorial Day weekend together, we walked and played with Gibbs and he seemed content.

But on the Fourth-of-July weekend, between grinding a tennis ball and bounding around a back pasture, a deer captured his attention, and he darted off through the back woods. There followed a few days (a couple of months in doggie time) of desperate searching for our lost dog. My distraught wife put 400 fliers in mailboxes around the countryside, spoke with dozens of empathetic neighbors, and wept. We drove into unexplored country roads, walked back woods, and posted signs. Finally, the dog sauntered to the back porch, exhausted, covered with pine pitch, and a bit nervous. Peri said that if I ever let him off leash again, she would tamper with my vitamins. She proceeded to call the dog "sweetheart," and began summoning me using doggie commands. I was no longer exactly sure where I fit in this neo-Freudian family structure.

Our biggest challenge was to accustom Gibbs to farmland littered with wandering chickens. He was an undersized Doberman and distinctly unaggressive, but roosters and guineas seemed to turn on a dormant switch. Gibbs could sit among hens while they calmly searched for insects, but he could not resist chasing guineas when they started to dash and lurch into low-lying branches. Once he offered me a guinea, held snuggly in his jaws, with a puzzled look that asked what his next move might be. He let the poor fowl loose, but never lost the instinctive drive to lunge after them. And although I cannot be sure, I suspect Gibbs was responsible for the deaths of a handful of roosters the one time I left him alone. A local tradesman told me what had happened on his grandpappy's farm when the family Doberman killed a chicken. Selling eggs was part of the family's livelihood, and the dog was immediately put down. There is no room for sentiment when survival is at stake, and the matter-of-fact reminiscence proved once again that I was not a serious farmer.

Within a year, Peri decided that Gibbs needed a sibling. We found another Doberman, this time closer to home. An alpha female, Danni had been crated for the entire first year of her life. She needed a few months of devotion to feel part of the family. It took her less time to prove she was heir apparent in the canine crew. Poor Gibbs let his new sister rule the house. Outside, Danni subjected Gibbs to a wily form of Greco-Roman wrestling. Danni was fifty percent larger than Gibbs, with lithe legs and childlike energy, and she easily maneuvered him into submission.

She was not so successful with the horse. Danni loved to dive under the paddock fence to dance around the retired stallion. Occasionally the horse, normally patient, would become aroused and start to prance, then run full throttle. The startled Doberman would dash across the pasture, stopping to gobble a mound of manure if there was time. Once, she threw herself back under the fence moments before the horse's rear legs thrust backwards to shatter one of the boards. Safely on the other side, Danni barked a meaningless warning. Whenever Gibbs was nearby, he would insert himself between Danni and the horse, running along the fence as her protector. I always felt sorry for him, for his bravery would soon be rewarded by more wrestling.

Ominous silences often alerted me to mischief, such as one dog or another poking its snout into a sluggish frog or a frightened baby copperhead. "It's hard to believe," advised the seasoned dog to the puppy in Allen Appel's playful *Old Dog's Guide for Pups*, "but not everyone wants to play." It was not long, however, before we experienced the most poignant moments of canine silence. Within one year, both of our Dobermans had to be put down. I found Gibbs resting in odd parts of the pastures, his energy level having plunged. He increasingly had trouble getting up on all fours. We would watch, helplessly, as he started to sprint after a squirrel, once one of his favorite games, only to stop mid-way to the tree. His cheeks started to swell, and we learned that he had developed a form of leukemia. When it became obvious that his pain was constant, I lifted him into the car into which he had once leaped to join his new family, and we drove off slowly to the veterinarian. Danni lay down next to him on the floor, eyes drooping, as a chemical concoction stopped Gibbs's heart.

A few months later, while waiting for Danni to make her quarter-mile sprint around the fenced perimeter, I heard a painful yelp across the woods. Running around one pasture and into the woods, I found her sprawled into a pile of leaves by a large trunk. I hoped that she had been bitten by a snake or had broken a leg—casualties that could be healed. Her front legs flailed, but she could not stand on her hind legs. The vet confirmed that she had broken her spine, which rendered her hind quarters paralyzed. Now both Gibbs and Danni lie buried in a corner of a fenced bit of woods, silent, just beyond the pasture where they had herded chickens and fended off hawks.

One of the most famous clues in detective fiction is "the dog that didn't bark in the night." The fact that a dog did not bark sparked the imagination of Sherlock Holmes, who solved the mystery of a missing racehorse, Silver Blaze, and the apparent murder of its trainer. Over two-and-a-half millennia earlier, Odysseus used the same analytical intelligence to determine whether an approaching stranger was friend or foe. The title for this chapter comes from one of my favorite lines in the *Odyssey.* It is a sentence that could never appear in a novel, but makes sense in an oral epic in which adjectives and noun pairs became part of a formula. The wine-dark sea, bright-eyed Athena, rosy-fingered dawn, and winged words are formulae that include familiar description while fitting into the verse meter. On occasion, the accompanying verb will render the sentence a bit unrealistic. "Barking dogs" is an oral formula, which could be followed by any verb, whether violent, playful, or passive. "The barking dogs were silent" may be jarring to those of us used to realistic prose, but audiences listening to Homeric bards would have taken it in stride.

Coming out of the herdsman Eumaios's hut, Odysseus noticed that the howling dogs suddenly fawned over a young man. Odysseus reasoned that the visitor must be a friend, not one of the evil suitors. "Eumaios, a friend of yours is on his way here," whispered Odysseus, "since the barking dogs are silent."

Before he revealed his identity to Eumaios, Odysseus encountered another silent dog. Argos, fabled for speed and hunting prowess in his youth, now lay motionless and abandoned atop a deep pile of dung. Too weak to move, he wagged his tail and laid both his ears back upon recognizing the master who had departed two decades ago. Before anyone else could notice his incipient excitement, Argos expired. Argos's silence was mixed with the pathos of death. It is one of the saddest moments in all of literature, sure to bring me to tears upon each reading. It is a miracle that Homer took so much care describing the end of a decrepit dog's life, a narrative interruption that slows the momentum of the heroic return of Odysseus to his wife and throne. It proves that however important the journey, or however clever the hero, our emotional life is what bestows upon us our humanity.

*To See a World in a Grain of Sand**

A wide diesel-fumed truck backed through the pasture toward the side of the barn. The driver opened the door and craned his neck, seeming unconcerned about the chickens who dashed toward his massive tires. When I signaled him to halt, he dumped a ton of Carolina river rock next to the barn.

The plot in front of the barn doors had started to look like an archaeological dig; whenever the sun shone, the chickens took advantage of dry dirt to dust-bathe. Their wings flurried in the dust, cleaning their feathers of mites and other parasites, In the process, they created craters the size of watermelons. When the clouds burst, the holes would fill.

River rock was my solution to the craters and their lakes. I plunged into the pile of rocks with a scoop shovel and spread them over a forty-square-yard plot. After a few loads I had to pause to catch my breath and allow the numbness of my forearms to retreat. Removing my cap and wiping my forehead with my sleeve, I felt a surge of relief, along with dizziness from standing erect too swiftly. Soon the world came back into focus, but in a new way. Moments ago, individual stones—medium-sized,

*From William Blake's poem "Auguries of Innocence"

yellow and gray—had captured my attention. Now, staring at the middle distance, my focus broadened to clusters of trees and earth sloping toward a creek. I always find beauty in the unique shapes of individual stones, and in the gentle way a tangerine tint morphs into bronze. But a different kind of beauty lies in a view of trees, water, and pastures that combine to imitate a painting of Poussin or Lorraine.

Around the time of the American Revolution, artist and travel writer William Gilpin promoted the idea of the picturesque in nature, a pre-Romantic concept that the eye creates the frame through which we view natural scenes. Thoreau mentioned Gilpin in *Walden* and admired him for his detailed descriptions and his broader, philosophical perspective. In his *Remarks on Forest Scenery, and Other Woodland Views (relative chiefly to picturesque beauty)*, Gilpin moved seamlessly from precise descriptions to thoughts on scenic beauty. When he came upon spruces while walking in Hampshire, England, he focused on their murky hue, irregular lateral branches, and feathery foliage. The sight prompted him to meditate on standards of beauty:

> The spruce fir is generally esteemed a more beautiful, and elegant tree, than the Scotch fir and the reason, I suppose, is, because it often feathers to the ground, and grows in a more exact, and regular shape. But this is a principal objection to it. It often wants both form and variety. We admire its floating foliage, in which it sometimes exceeds all other trees; but it is rather disagreeable to see a repeti-

> tion of these feathery strata, beautiful as they are, reared, tier above tier, in regular order, from the bottom of a tree to the top.

Gilpin's mental lens focused on tree branches and colors but quickly faded back to capture entire trees. He felt the wide shot provided the basis for picturesque beauty and invited meditation on composite natural scenes. A chasm opened between my close focus on an individual stone's striations and the meditative view that captures the artistic beauty in a scene as a whole. My mind can shift between the strategies but cannot juggle both simultaneously.

Appreciating the beauty in landscapes, whether in microscopic details or spatial views, became possible only relatively recently. It was not until the eighteenth and nineteenth centuries that artists could imagine painting a landscape for its intrinsic beauty without suggesting theological layers of meaning. Augustine posited the doctrine that objects in nature signify something about their Creator, a theological view that dominated Western thinking for over a millennium. Petrarch was one of the first writers to try to escape Augustine's pull and desacralize nature. In his epistle "The Ascent of Mont Ventoux" he sought poetic inspiration in nature's wonders. One of the early climbers of Provence's "windy peak," Petrarch wanted to promote a new way of thinking that escaped theological shackles dating from the Middle Ages. He wanted to enjoy the mountain for its own sake, not as a symbol of a religious journey as it had been in Dante. (In another challenge to "authority," he placed higher value on an individual's solitary meditation than on friendship—thereby rejecting Aristotle's view that friendship was the highest virtue of all.)

But while gazing at the horizon, in one direction toward Marseilles and in another toward the Rhône, Petrarch consulted a copy of Augustine's *Confessions*. Suddenly the ascent took on a negative moral valence, for the book opened at random to a passage that condemned men who admired high mountains. Mountain climbing to appreciate nature suddenly became a temporary, sinful moment in a pilgrim's progress, and Petrarch ultimately condemned his own moral failure. Apparently, freedom to appreciate natural beauty in detail has not been available at every cultural moment.

Like Petrarch, Thoreau also retreated from an awed appreciation of nature's beauty, although for a different reason. In his early essay "A Walk to Wachusett," he was aware of achieving the heights of the mountain and marveled at the view a migrating bird might take, easily navigating between the Green Mountains and the ocean. But the ascent was accompanied by reading Virgil and Wordsworth on the one hand and musing about the spot of Mrs. Rowlandson's capture by Indians in the 1670s on the other. The religious and romantic imagination cannot easily see nature without cultural baggage.

Many Enlightenment naturalists finally enabled us to see nature directly, but let me quote the greatest of these. In 1833, Darwin rode into the Brazilian forest from the shores of Bahia Blanca "curious to observe how far from the parent rock any pebbles could be found." Starting from the pebbles on the shore, he rode toward a large quarry of quartz forty-five miles inland.

As he traveled to the mountains, Darwin noticed the whitish gray of the rock fragments. The next day he ascended a ridge but was disappointed with the mundane view of the pass below. He climbed yet another peak, "and every purpose of geology had been answered. . . . I do not doubt these pebbles were in a similar manner aggregated, at a period when the great calcareous formation was depositing beneath the surrounding sea." This journal entry in *Voyage of the Beagle* was a turning point in the history of the human eye. Darwin looked carefully at rocks, not as a sign of God's intrusion into our world and not as an opportunity for the imagination to muse upon literary and historical ancestors. Instead, he observed the color and striation of quartz to map the geological course of the rocks themselves.

For my part, I returned to observing the individual stones in my shovel. There were dozens of patterns of erosion and striations of color. Having endured millennia of river currents, the stones were rounded, but each had a unique ovoid shape, and each displayed a distinctive mix of beige, yellow, and burnt orange depending upon where it had broken off from a larger rock. As I lugged another load of Carolina river rock, sweat dripped from my forehead onto the shovel and brightened the earth tones of the rocks. I was registering mundane, even trivial observations. But they were observations I could have made only after Darwin trekked up a mountain in Brazil.

Fable of the Bees

An aggressive buzzing around the house disturbed a peaceful autumn afternoon. Upon investigating, I found dried mud-daubed cylinders, resembling tiny organ pipes fitted snuggly between the cedar shingles. I feared a wasp infestation. Hugging the corner of the house as I crept toward the source of the noise, I spied instead a rotund bee. Poised mid-air, it started to vibrate like a berserker, the legendary old Norse warriors who fought in a trance-like fury. Then it carved a circular entrance into the shingles with its mandible. My first home repair would be filling in holes drilled by a single carpenter bee.

I soon lost sight of that bee but felt sure it could make a home in any one of the dozens of hickories, oaks, or maples on our property. I felt less sanguine about the absence of honey bees on the property, and about the pollinator crisis that threatened a third of the national food supply. Apiculture had never seen such an extensive colony collapse. Everything seemed to conspire against bees: the predominance of decorative flowers over native species; climate change; neuro-toxic insecticides (neonicotinoids); and parasites. The pesticides alone impaired bee mobility, navigation, feeding behavior, foraging activity, memory, and learning. To respond to the crisis, I decided that my first landscaping project would be to replace two thousand square feet of grass, circled by a driveway, with a field of pollinator plants.

Peri suggested flowering herbs to nourish the dwindling population of bees. I experimented with thyme because my favorite honey came from the mountains of Crete, where bees frolicked among the purple flowers of the native herb. Thyme has an ancient lineage on the Greek island, where it has been used for medicinal purposes, in restorative teas, for honey production, as well as for flavoring in traditional Greek fare. Ancient Greek texts, from Linear B tablets to Hesiod's *Works and Days* to Athenaeus's *Deipnosophists*, attested to its usefulness. Nostalgic for my cultural roots, I wanted to transplant the Greek curative and culinary herb to my own landscape to jump-start a honey bee colony.

I uprooted and raked the large circle of grass. Since the sterile ground would have been inhospitable to any flower trying to take root, I paid a dump truck to drop four tons of topsoil onto the spot. For several hours I raked the pyramid into gently rolling folds. Then, like the sower in a Millet painting, I tossed thyme seeds as I zigzagged about the small field. The seeds were almost microscopic, and I struggled to space them according to the directions on the package.

My impatience resulted in clumps of seeds sown in the barren soil. It took several weeks for the tiniest growth to appear. The bed's bald pate slowly transformed into ungainly patches, and ultimately into a large, luxurious swath of green. In future plots I learned to mix seeds in buckets of soil or sand and to fling the mixture more evenly.

It took more weeks to see purple hints of a flower. Finally, they blossomed in profusion, and a swarm of bees began to hover. Musing over the hours of shoveling, hoeing, and planting that created the thyme garden, I decided that patience had been my greatest virtue in the months leading from seed to sprout. Patience is a virtue more at home in the *New Testament* than in the *Iliad*. *Macro-themia,* literally great passion or long suffering, was one of the virtues to which Paul directed the Galatians. Nietzsche derided it, and it was not my strong suit. But nature demanded it.

Watching a bee alight on a purple blossom, my mind wandered back four decades to the times I took my maternal grandmother, Cleopatra, to Spili, her native village in Crete. There, I discovered that bees connected me to the world of my ancestors. In my drives through the Cretan mountains, I spotted rows of small cubical beehives. They wound around distant, isolated ridges, like evidence of an abandoned civilization. I had seen beekeepers remove the cover of the boxes and lift hanging squares, patterned with honeyed hexagons. And local grocery store shelves were laden with jars of Cretan thyme honey.

My grandmother told me that as a child she listened eagerly for the arrival of the beekeeper in the village. Her ear was finely attuned to the sounds of Mount Vorizi, the mountain into which Spili is nestled; to the underground spring gushing into the communal washing basin down the path; to the wind tumbling from the summit into the valley; to the bells clanging on the necks of sheep and goats.

To the young Cleopatra this music of the mountain air was as commonplace as moonlight. But the din of a single bell was startling, a prophet announcing something rare and special—the arrival of the beekeeper. When she and the other young children of the village heard that distinctive lone bell, shaken by the regular and sturdy steps of the beekeeper's donkey, they left their domestic chores to meet him.

The beekeeper's donkey lugged clay jars filled with honeycomb strapped over its sides. The jars, as tall as some of the smaller children, were shaped like miniature Minoan *pithoi*. Each had ear-like clay handles and a thin lip that flared outward at the top. The beekeeper kept the lip filled with water so that ants would drown in their relentless pursuit of the honey. He also carried amber bars of honeycomb that looked like waxy, aerated bars of gold—the same kind of bars that had been sold in Byzantine markets centuries earlier. The children of Spili would run up the mountain path to meet him and he would break off small pieces of honeycomb for them. The children would suck them until they emptied them of every viscous drop. Then they would chew the remnants of honeycomb like gum until it dissolved. According to my grandmother, these village taste testers always smiled in approval, and led the beekeeper in an ecstatic, Eleusinian procession into the village.

The buzzing in my thyme garden swelled, drawing my mind back from Crete and warning me of the dangers of standing in the midst of the bees. I walked toward the porch, mulling over how I could create an even larger bee empire. That afternoon I contacted the government experts in Hillsborough, recently named the thirty-fifth American bee city (the first bee city was Asheville, North Carolina). A few phone calls later, I was in touch with a local beekeeper, a fellow armed with a Ph.D. in organic chemistry and an inventory of over 100 million bees.

Jeff, a short and sturdy man, drove up the driveway and bounced out of his old white Toyota, eager to tour our pastures. He scoured the tree lines and traced out the sun's path to identify a plot with enough sunlight to battle the parasites that were plaguing his hives. We settled on an elevated corner of a pasture behind the barn, far from marauding chickens.

A few days later he returned with a large flat-bed truck and a forklift. He used a fleet of equipment to transport his bees—to California to pollinate almond orchards, to Maine to pollinate blueberry bushes, to the mountains of western North Carolina to survive the dry, hot summer, and to pastures like mine to gather pollen. Most of his income, he told me, came not from honey but from farmers renting his bees for stud service.

His twelve-wheeler truck was laden with several pallets of bee boxes that housed one and a half million bees. The tires carved out trenches as the truck crawled around a tuft of trees toward the designated corner of the pasture. Jeff then leapt out, started the fork lift, and maneuvered pallets filled with white boxes into a circle at the end of the open acre. After lowering the final pallet into position, he left his bees to collect pollen from my fields and woods, which boast plenty of poplar and other blossoming trees for pollination.

Jeff, who called himself a bee shepherd, came to the bee pasture every couple of weeks to inspect the hives. One day he arrived fully clad, a knight in white armor and helmet, and sprayed a mixture of oxalic acid and powdered sugar to reduce the varroa mite population. Meanwhile, I bush-hogged the pasture. Warrior bees swarmed around Jeff and pursued me until I rode a safe distance away from their boxes.

After my day of bush-hogging on the bee pasture, I collapsed on the couch and drifted toward sleep while reading Kazantzakis's epic, *The Odyssey: A Modern Sequel*. Exhausted from my chores, I lingered over stunning images of plows and pomegranates, of bees and furrowed fields, and of fertile seeds. But moments of intensely felt lyrical beauty were darkened by scenes of psychological torment. Odysseus landed on Crete after rescuing Helen from her drunken husband, Menelaus. Moving inland from the Minoan harbor to destroy Knossos, he plotted to assassinate the senile king Idomeneus, who harbored incestuous yearnings for his daughter. On the way, Odysseus told his companions that his breast was "a buzzing beehive of unruly bees, and I don't know as yet just when the bees will swarm."

The final moments of Odysseus's father were darker still. Laertes staggered, fell, and dragged himself on shaking knees, clawing the ground until his beard caked with mud. Having returned home after hours in the fields, I empathized with Laertes.

Scholarly Footnote

The beekeeper, like the farmer, belongs to a classical poetic genre called the georgic, almost forgotten since its last resurgence in the eighteenth century. The georgic, as its Greek root suggests, locates virtue in the land (as opposed to the newer urban centers of civilization), and glories in details of the landscape. It elevates the primitive, unsophisticated virtues of rustics and plowmen and beekeepers and creates a moral hierarchy of religious and civic virtues. Aelian writes about bees in order to praise loyalty to kings, civic industriousness, temperance, and courage. Hesiod, in the course of offering advice about farming, boosts piety, moderation, practicality, respect for elders, obedience, thrift, reserved speech, and hospitality. And the greatest of these is hard work. In the sweat of the georgic farmer, and of the beekeeper, lay the repository of ancient virtue.

Bees rose to Western literary prominence in Virgil's *Georgics,* one of the most popular works of classical literature for almost two thousand years. In the fourth book of the poem he explained how to know when bees begin to gather honey, how to call them home when they swarm, and how to part them when they engage in battle. The poem sometimes verges on the epic, as when he compares bees with mythic and Roman heroes who defended their kings and cities in battle. But the poem always returns to the tonic chord of rustic virtue. Their modest appetite, sang the poet, keeps them chaste, their work ethic builds waxen cities, their civic virtue produces ambrosial dews.

Virgil's *Georgics* was translated by Dryden and imitated by Pope. Dryden, like Montaigne, called it the best poem of the best poet. Only a few prose works of the last few centuries belong to the ancient genre: the Jeffersonian era's vision of an agricultural utopia produced Hector St. John de Crèvecoeur's *Letters from an American Farmer*; *Walden* is a georgic record of self-sufficiency, a retreat from the city, and careful tending of seedlings; Cather chose an epigram from the third book of the *Georgics* for *My Ántonia*, where understated heroic endurance in the farmland harkened back to Virgil and Hesiod. On a smaller but charming scale, Betty MacDonald's *The Egg and I* chronicled a year in the life of a hardworking wife tending chickens, raising vegetables, and other farm chores.

In the English tradition the link between bees, hard work, and economics goes back to Mandeville, whose poem "The Fable of the Bees: or Private Vices, Public Benefits" evoked moral outrage at the outset of the eighteenth century. Three-quarters of a century before Adam Smith's *Wealth of Nations*, the poem helped introduce the division of labor and the invisible hand. But it was, according to Keynes, "convicted as a nuisance by the grand jury of Middlesex in 1723" because it linked prosperity with greed and claimed that vicious human desires created civilization. One century later, bees became the focus of scientific rather than moral enquiry. Among Emerson's readings in natural philosophy in the 1830s were Huber's *New Observations of Bees* and Spence's four-volume *Introduction to Entomology*.

Varieties of Religious Experience: Second Meditation

I trudged to the barn on a Sunday morning and realized I had not taken a day off in a few months. I wondered about the fact that ancient farmers of the various Abrahamic religions observed weekly cycles that contained six days of labor and one day of leisure and prayer. Islam's day of rest is Friday. The Jewish Sabbath is Saturday. Christians typically attend church services on Sunday. My day of leisure and prayer had been delayed for several months.

My life on the farm resembled ritual but did not lend itself to patterns of work and leisure. Branches do not stop falling, chickens do not stop eating (or pooping), grass does not stop growing. I have found that working every day can barely prevent chaos from coming again. I have confessed in these chapters to a manic response to work in the woods and fields. I have ridden the pendulum swing between melancholy and wonder, between despair and joy.

Many observers have described joy in the language of religious awe. I have already quoted Darwin, who ends his masterpiece with a lyrical hymn to nature:

> There is grandeur in this view of life, with its several powers, having been originally breathed by

> the Creator into a few forms or into one; and that, whilst this planet has gone cycling on according to the fixed law of gravity, from so simple a beginning endless forms most beautiful and most wonderful have been, and are being, evolved.

In a more magical forest, the beeches, oaks, and pines give Mary Oliver "such hints of gladness" that they instill in her a personal sense of redemption in her poem "When I am Among the Trees."

After my first annual cycle on the farm it dawned on me that the spiritual awe that nature inspired in Darwin and Oliver could be mapped onto ancient religious tenets. Each Abrahamic faith asks its congregations to attend to three religious pillars: ritual, or the liturgy; theological writings; and the mystical tradition. I have tried to honor each of these aspects in my meditations on the farm.

The liturgy is a weekly, if not daily, ritual that brings communities together. The Byzantine Orthodox liturgy, to take one example, is a drama that celebrates the life and sacrifice of the Son of God. It is at once historical, alluding to the Last Supper, Crucifixion, and Resurrection, and cyclical—the drama repeats every week, and the cycle of biblical texts repeats annually.

Theological niceties are embodied in the Nicene Creed, which is incorporated into the drama written by St. John Chrysostom (there are other versions by St. Basil and others). Debates about the the two axes of theological thought, the nature of the Trinity and the divine-human nature of Christ, are settled in the creed. Theology also incorporates the rules of religious life—

the sacraments, the customs, the habits developed during a life of cyclically repeating the Jesus prayer and hymns to the Mother of God, fasts, and biblical readings.

Rituals and rules are easier to grasp than mysticism, the third pillar of Greek Orthodoxy. A powerful movement away from strict theology and toward mysticism began at the end of the Byzantine Empire, at a time of great prosperity, when many of the monks wanted to return to a more ascetic and primitive Christianity. These monks turned their backs on worldly affairs, leaving the administration in the hands of the much less qualified lower ranks of civil servants. They started a new spiritual movement, which became known as Hesychasm, from the Greek word *hesychia*, meaning quietness. This form of mysticism penetrated all aspects of religious life, including the painting of icons, which became more emotionally powerful and psychologically moving.

The champion of Hesychasm, Gregory of Palamas, the Archbishop of Thessalonica, defended the mystical practice in his *Triads in Defense of the Holy Hesychasts*. He rigorously defended prayer as central to Eastern Christianity and insisted that the mystic focus was on the heart. Most importantly for the Church, he acknowledged that believers could approach union with God through the liturgy as well as through mysticism.

These three pillars, ritual, theology, and mysticism, have their counterparts on the farm. First, there is the cyclical nature of the landscape—the seasons, the constellations, the rotation of colors, the annual cycle of tasks, and so on. Like religious ritual, nature's cycles offer a sense of consistency, even of peace. They are proof of the existence of something more powerful than mere humans.

Second, there are the rules that farmers have developed over the centuries. Hesiod in Greece, Cato the Rustic and Virgil in Rome, and dozens of their agriculturalist descendants have codified procedures of tilling, planting, and harvesting. Like theological niceties, the necessary work of each season requires study, contemplation, and practice.

Finally, there is the magic that pervades the land: the Impressionist shimmering of blue shadows; the miracle of buds sprouting after ice storms; the beauty of fuchsia, apricot, and lavender petals. Botany can explain stamens and pistils, and chemistry can plot the molecular workings of photosynthesis and the flow of nutrients in the mycelial network, but scientific tomes only increase the mystery described by Dylan Thomas as "the force that through the green fuse drives the flower."

The South

Communitarians

I looked up from nailing a few loosened fence planks at the far end of Oliver's pasture and spotted a coyote lurking behind the barn. His dull white fur, stained with dark threads, had thickened in the early winter months. The creature had stalked out of the woods, crouched, and paused as it took in the geometry of the attack: the trajectory of the leap over the fence, the wide flanking swing toward the horse, and the escape route. I in turn calculated the probability that the predator was hungry and daring enough to attack. I hung my hammer on the fence, angry that I had not brought my shotgun.

Fellow farmers had warned me about coyotes coming through the woods. One neighbor told me that packs were especially dangerous. He had watched as a female lured his dog into the woods as her companions swooped into a flock of chickens. He also advised me to obtain a donkey, a species known to be fiercely protective. Their wide range of vision and steadiness in the face of threats make them valuable herders. Unfortunately, they consider dogs a threat to horses, and a swift kick would prove fatal.

As I stilled myself and focused on the coyote, I glanced at a wandering troop of guinea fowl. They left their pecking and fussing, their necks stretched upward like periscopes, and their heads turned sideways to examine the beast. In concert, they marched toward Oliver, flew a dozen yards to perch on the fence, and dropped to the ground to form an elliptical curve. Then they began to chase the coyote.

The coyote was more lumbering than lithe, but it could have easily gobbled any single guinea at will. It had no strategy, however, against twelve guineas circling and herding it back into the woods.

These guineas had seen seven of their colleagues lanced by hawks and beheaded by owls. As individuals, they each scattered under the closest bush when threat loomed. But when together, the communitarian instinct overcame a mortal threat. A band of bite-sized guineas overcame a hungry coyote. It was a protective group of guineas that drew Darwin's admiration when he trekked in the Cape de Verd Islands. "Near Fuentes," he wrote in his journal, "we saw a large flock of guinea-fowl—probably fifty or sixty in number. They were extremely wary, and could not be approached. They avoided us, like partridges on a rainy day in September, running with their heads cocked up; and if pursued, they readily took to the wing."

The coordinated military strategy executed by the troop of guineas put me in mind of a famous cultural history of the South, W. J. Cash's *Mind of the South*. Contemporary with *Gone with the Wind*, Cash's book investigated the southern class system and legacy of racism, and pinpointed dominant character traits that have remained constant throughout the sweep of Southern history: evangelical fervor; the honor code that prescribed violence as a cure for conflict; a stubborn stance against law and government; a tendency toward unreality and romanticism; and idolatry of women and female virtue. These values have persisted through the centuries, from Jamestown's landed gentry and bonded servants to colonial and antebellum plantations to Confederate romantics and onward through the periods of Reconstruction, Redeemers, Jim Crow, and industrialization.

Informing each of these southern values was a fierce individualism. It was not the forward-looking individualism of Emerson, who sought to free Americans from the gravitational pull of Europe. It was not individualism as commonly understood in the North, a rugged independence constrained by urban forces and a sense of social responsibility. It was a backward-looking individualism, nourished on the frontier and nurtured on the isolated plantation. Child labor laws, public schools, roads, and other social institutions were vigorously contested in the post-bellum South. As a southerner, Cash seemed deeply troubled by the backwardness, oppression, pieties, myths, and inhumanity of his culture's version of individualism.

After the guineas forced the coyote to retreat from Oliver's pasture, they returned to their repast of insects. They roamed, some in small groups, others in individual pursuit. I watched as a blue-gray pied guinea chased an African white, with no apparent motive. The latter hopped a couple of feet in a flurry of color, came back to earth, then scampered in long elliptical curves. Her colleagues seemed oblivious to her plight.

Eventually, the flurry and bobbing ceased, and the entire flock marched a hundred yards in lockstep out of the pasture and toward their barn. I mused how easily they seemed to move between exhibiting a playful individualism and acting as a solemn and protective band of brothers and sisters.

Of Statues and Graves

An old, pale green station wagon pulled into our driveway with blue bins huddled against every window. A man balancing a stack of egg cartons slowly emerged from a creaky door and then bounded up the brick steps to the front door. Michael was a founding member of Piedmont Progressive Farms, an agricultural cooperative centered in Yanceyville, halfway between Hillsborough and the Virginia border. The cooperative, which had started as a small group of Black farmers, had broadened its outreach, as Michael and his colleagues recruited minority, disadvantaged, or, in our case, inexperienced farmers to contribute to their output of beef, chicken, fruits, vegetables, and eggs.

Our first cohort of chicks started laying on New Year's Eve. The early weeks of January yielded two small eggs every other day, enough for a small order of scrambled eggs. By March, as egg production increased, we grew tired of omelets and frittatas. Whenever we visited friends that spring, we offloaded a couple of cartons, a gift from our generous hens. By June, Peri had a business plan to deal with our excess supply.

First, she enrolled in a course from a local university agriculture department, where she learned to candle, wash, and disinfect our daily pail of eggs. Second, she marketed our eggs to several stores and cooperatives. Piedmont Progressive Farms was curious. Although we had little to offer them (a minuscule percentage of their weekly egg production and less expertise), they were looking for pasture-fed and free-range egg farmers. Michael, as eager as he was welcoming, invited us into the cooperative. He arrived at our house every week with cartons to fill and delivered our eggs to a local market.

Although he and his fellow entrepreneurs had grown up on farms, they had all built formidable careers, with executive positions at Duke Energy, Diebold, the New York City Department of Corrections, and the Army. Returning to their childhood farms, they had dedicated themselves to helping farmers develop skills and find markets. Despite their impressive resumes, they came across as humble workers of the earth, eager to brainstorm about what to grow or how to increase production.

In the months before Peri and I left Manhattan for the Piedmont section of North Carolina, two articles had appeared in the national press about race relations in the South. The first was about the plight of Black farmers. The number of acres of land farmed by African American families had plummeted over the previous century, due in part to urbanization but also to violence, lynching, and racist laws. Black farmers currently made up only about one percent of the country's producers.

The second article explained the controversy over a building that had opened in 1934 as the Confederate Memorial Library in Hillsborough. Almost half a century later, the word "library" was removed from the chiseled beam above the entrance. Then, in 2015, the Orange County Commissioners voted to replace "Confederate Memorial" with "County Historical Museum" on the architrave. After decades of complacency, historical inertia, and Lost Cause nostalgia, the vote was met with fierce opposition.

There was a factual objection to the old name—namely, that there were few items in the museum that had anything to do with the Confederacy. The exhibits did include Civil War drumsticks found at Gettysburg, engravings of Hillsboro Academy and the surrender at Bennett Place, and a canteen and nurse uniform. But they were surrounded by furniture from the eighteenth century, weights and measures, baseball memorabilia, tools of the cotton industry, tobacco paraphernalia, items from the Regulators, and much more. Factual observations like these, however, held little sway in the emotionally charged debate about ancestors and historical identity.

When I toured the historical museum several months after my arrival in Hillsborough, I told the museum director that the decision to remove the offending words contributed to my decision to move nearby. She smiled shyly and told me under her breath that she was the one who requested the name change. She and several of the county commissioners had subsequently received threatening phone calls. Town officials anticipated civil unrest on the day the building was to be officially baptized with its new name.

The director's smile broadened as she told me about the re-opening. Black citizens, including one commissioner, came to the museum for the first time. They had felt unwelcome at best, and threatened at worst, with the Confederate moniker. Here lies the most suppressed aspect of such historical and moral debates in the South. Loyal descendants of Confederates insist that their allegiance to warrior ancestors justifies continued worship of the Old South. At the same time, and with the same energy, they deflect the painful awareness that other family trees have their roots in chattel slavery.

I would like to linger on the metaphor of the family tree. Hierarchical charts with husbands linked to wives and offspring below lose the organic vigor of the original image. Expanding downwards through the generations, they also sacrifice the notion of roots. Roots are mostly invisible but have awe-inspiring power—to battle the force of gravity to draw gallons of water and nutrients upward, to break through rocks and cement pipes, to balance and support several tons of bark and branch. To revivify the root metaphor in the context of Southern history, I put forth the fact that white and Black family roots have often become inextricably confused, as male masters raped or sexually coerced female slaves.

Many southern Black lineages have their family trees rooted with the same Confederate officers as those who continue to honor their statues and flag. Just such genetic heritage underlies the historical tragedy of *Light in August* and other Faulkner novels. It partly explains the famous quip in *Requiem for a Nun*: "The past is never dead. It's not even past."

Three decades later, another American author riffed on Faulkner's apparent paradox about history, this time amidst the struggle for civil rights, explicitly pinning it on the corrosive effect of repressing America's "appallingly oppressive and bloody history" on white consciousness. In an essay entitled "The White Man's Guilt," James Baldwin wrote that

> History, as nearly no one seems to know, is not merely something to be read. And it does not refer merely, or even principally, to the past. On the contrary, the great force of history comes from the fact that we carry it within us, are unconsciously controlled by it in many ways, and history is literally *present* in all that we do. It could scarcely be otherwise, since it is to history that we owe our frames of reference, our identities, and our aspirations.

Walking in the woods always invited me to muse about the life force of mycelial networks and roots. But I began this thought process with a historical issue, and that has led me to the dark, disturbing, and violent energy of roots. It also led me to think about local underground detritus, or I should say historical remains. In my woods there are rolling mounds and sinuous trenches, which an American historian has identified as Civil War earthworks. Confederate soldiers bivouacked here toward the end of the war. Sherman marched on a nearby trail after his victory over Johnston at Bentonville, the last major battle of the war. The mounds are a reminder of the fact that although North Carolina had fewer plantations and fewer slaves than most Southern states, slaves still accounted for one-third of the population of the county.

After Sherman marched through Hillsborough, he passed by a church cemetery where one of the South's fiercest defenders of slavery lies buried. Thomas Ruffin was an antebellum North Carolina Supreme Court Justice. He is notorious for his 1830 opinion in *State v. Mann*, a decision in which he justified Mann's beating and shooting of a female slave named Lydia. "The power of the master must be absolute," wrote Ruffin, "to render the submission of the slave perfect." Slavery had been founded on violence, and violence was necessary to maintain the institution. Profit and the safety of the slaveholder trumped law and liberal principles.

The law, for Ruffin, left no room for sentiment or conscience or humane treatment. He lamented, at the beginning of his opinion, that the slave's humanity may appeal to the man, but the magistrate must objectively apply the law. But to arrive at the law (that is, that violence may be necessary to support the institution of slavery), Ruffin assumed the inequality of slave and master. He made the further assumption that slavery must continue to underwrite the profits of the plantation owner. It is not surprising that the argument led ineluctably to the conclusion that the slave had no legal recourse.

Abolitionist and author of *Uncle Tom's Cabin*, Harriet Beecher Stowe admired the clarity of Ruffin's argument, however much she despised the cruelty. I am more cynical, given that the legal sleight of hand allowed Ruffin to arrive right back at his assumptions. His legal opinion is a prominent antebellum example of begging the question masquerading as objective, logical reasoning instead of the legerdemain it is.

Ruffin's opinion overturned the trial court's decision against Mann and cemented the positivist interpretation of the law of slavery for the three decades that preceded Fort Sumter. Despite that fact, or perhaps because of it, there is a statue of Ruffin in an alcove of the State Court of Appeals building in Raleigh. It has not yet received the attention of statues of other Confederate icons in the area, such as Silent Sam or Robert E. Lee or Jefferson Davis.

Faulkner invited us to meditate on the power of Confederate statues in the final scene of *The Sound and the Fury*, when the impish Luster tried to change Benjy's comfortable routine. From the Compsons' home, the route to the cemetery, which holds Benjy's father and brother, proceeded through the center of Jefferson and around a circular path, at the center of which stood a marble soldier atop a column. Instead of leading the horses to the right as usual, Luster urged them leftward. Benjy predictably descended into hysterics.

For the idiot, repetition was required for a peaceful day, and the dark side of repetition is being shackled to the past. Driving right along the circle was comforting to Benjy, but as a historical allegory it signaled two disturbing ideas. First, it meant that some folk must travel counterclockwise, emblematically moving backwards in time. Second, given that Benjy's neck had to be turned to the left, it meant that he looked away from the series of houses and toward the center of the circle and the Confederate statue. Idiots in Faulkner's world, those unable to resist the gravitational pull of Bull Run, Shiloh, and Gettysburg, move in circles, unable to look away from the Civil War, staring at the past in general and specifically the Southern, heroic version of the war and its concomitant racial resentments.

Ruffin's burial plot in Hillsborough, as opposed to his statue in Raleigh, contains the remains of the actual man and has become part of the landscape. The grave has an organic connection to us. For me, it is a much more permanent and powerful reminder than his statue is of the violence he codified into law. It remains an underground force, a reminder that we can never eradicate the sort of rationalizations of inequality that Ruffin once institutionalized. As Annette Clapsaddle remarked in her novel *Even as We Breathe*, "what is buried in the ground isn't always what you think."

Given the violence and injustices perpetrated against Africans and African Americans, the brotherhood and empathy extended to me by local tradesfolk, many of them Black, has surprised me since my arrival in the South. I do not claim that there is no evidence of historical resentment, just that I have noticed overwhelming kindness and generosity. The itinerant mower mechanic, Rick, spends as much time exchanging witticisms with me as he does tinkering with belts and blades and oil filters. He is as earthy as he is engaging, and he is unfailingly patient with my ignorance of engines. The stone mason we hired noticed my exasperation at a previous incomplete roof repair and went out of his way to waterproof an expansive chimney as well as to caulk unreachable (to me) bricks under the sloping attic roof. His calming and professional demeanor seemed to me driven as much by a tradition of hospitality as by a tradesman's care in his work.

In praising this sort of kindness, I fear I have become a parody of a northern liberal. I don't wish to be the kind of northerner whom Florence King made fun of in *Southern Ladies and Gentlemen*, the kind of person who is awestruck at the Samaritan who goes out of his way to be of service and who gushes with "effusions along the lines of 'I didn't think there were people like that left!'"

But the feeling of moral renewal I felt with my initial encounters with the mower repair man and the stone mason never dulled or softened into commonplace, scripted encounters. Like Walt Whitman, my landscape is filled with the song of the carpenter, the mason, and the farmer. "I'll sing for them," chanted Shelby Stephenson, in his poem "How We Lived," "for the factory workers, tobacco primers, string-loopers, truck drivers (wheels and slides)." These tradesmen, and the farmers from our agricultural cooperative, have added richness to our new lives. I hope they are among those who have felt welcomed by the newly christened County Historical Museum.

Road Trips, Southern Style: Third Meditation

Crouching on a boulder after an hour of hacking into a patch of clay, I swiped my forehead with a handkerchief and patted the sting from my eyes. When the world came back into focus, I gazed at a kaleidoscope of colored feathers dancing before the barn. Groups of polka-dotted black feathers, rosy-tan feathers, iridescent green feathers, all in constant motion. The rocking action mesmerized me. The chickens made two rapid swipes with a claw, moved mechanically backwards in one step, then dove into the earth to snap up a tick, pierce a beetle, or wrestle a worm. The sideways turn of the neck, to view the ground with one red eye, resembled the focused glare of raptors in *Jurassic Park*.

Hens lead double lives, alternately as individualists and communitarians. When they scratch for insects, they remain intensely focused, oblivious to their colleagues. They are more social when they scratch basin-like holes for their dust bath rituals. Their claws can dig deep enough into hardened clay to bury half of their feathered bulk in a dusty hole. There they can lie and wriggle for hours in the loosened soil, dust-bathing their feathers and cleansing themselves of parasites in the process. Half a dozen hens lie quietly together, like a wine club in a sauna. After sunning themselves for a leisurely portion of the afternoon, they shake their feathers and saunter off together. They can transform a lush and level green lawn into a potted field of weed tufts over a couple summer months.

When dust-bathing holes transform a pasture into a moonscape, I attempt to repair the damage to the landscape. Trudging with hammer and wrenches to the open shed where I store a tractor, I stare at all the levers necessary to connect the tiller to the machine. I make several attempts to back the tractor into the tiller, so that the points of attachment were tantalizingly close. I'm a novice at anything mechanical, and afraid of crushing my fingers. It takes me at least fifteen minutes to align the heavy metal rods with the tiller joints and wrestle the tractor and cotter pins into place. My dungarees are drenched by the time I manage to attach the bar for the hydraulic lift and finally the drive shaft.

As I haul myself up to the tractor seat, perch over the steering wheel, and engage the tiller, hens and roosters are drawn to the front tires. Chickens are bizarrely attracted to moving vehicles and loud whirring noises. A hen will walk in front of a moving tractor in order to get out of its way. A rooster will stare down a tractor until it breathes diesel fumes. Otherwise, they seem to love machines at rest—groups of them will sun themselves in the driver's seat and poop on the hood. Tilling the ground unearths the weeds and partially levels the holes. Chickens dash to the newly furrowed earth for signs of insects in distress.

Hard work, long ago identified by Max Weber as a

core component of the Puritan vision,* belongs in the realm of Protestant ethics and underwrites many of the measures of success: owning a home, upward mobility, education, and equal opportunity. As Edward Winslow of Plymouth Plantation noted, "In America, religion and profit jump together."† It was the comingling of philosophical and Yankee values that inspired Marius Bewley to define the American dream as the "romantic enlargement of the possibilities of life on a level at which the material and the spiritual have become inextricably confused."‡ Given the oxymoronic combinations of liberty and equality, individualism and democracy, and freedom of conscience and accumulation of wealth that complicate the definition of the American dream, we may well have to throw up our hands and co-opt the fearless assertion of Walt Whitman, "Do I contradict myself? Very well then I contradict myself, (I am large, I contain multitudes.)"§

In rural North Carolina, situated in the lower upper South, I'm considered a damned Yankee, that is, a carpetbagger who traveled south of the Mason-Dixon line and settled. I followed in the wake of two famous travelers. De Tocqueville went down the Ohio and Mississippi rivers to New Orleans, later making his way to Washington through the South. He spotted volumes of Shake-

*Max Weber's *The Protestant Ethic and the Spirit of Capitalism*

†Edward Winslow, chapter 8 of *Good News from New England*

‡From Marius Bewley's chapter "Scott Fitzgerald and the Collapse of the American Dream" in *The Eccentric Design*

§From Walt Whitman's "Song of Myself"

speare and Milton in a cabin near Memphis; he saw a band of Choctaw Indians, including "an old woman more than 120 years of age," forcibly being removed from their homeland; he visited a cotton plantation. Of the white man, the Native American, and the slave, de Tocqueville asked: "Why is it that of these three races, one was born to perish, one to rule, and one to serve?"*

Two decades later, Frederick Law Olmsted, before he became a landscape architect, traveled through the Deep South as a journalist. He argued that although moral arguments against slavery were compelling, economic arguments predicted the downfall of the Cotton Kingdom: one-crop agriculture, the lack of infrastructure and industry, and the reliance on imports all conspired to precipitate a political crisis.

Part of my cultural baggage is a northern sense of American history and a weighty dose of Puritan values. My northern values of thrift, busy-ness, hard work, and subsequent upward social mobility—standard components of the American dream—often seem out of place. The pace is often much slower in the South, people in the trades are not typically in a hurry to return your phone call or indeed to show up at appointed times, and leisure is valued more highly than in the North. Farmers work long hours, but often strive just to keep economically even. As I re-read American novels (and discover many Southern ones), I am jolted into the recognition that the American dream has distinctly northern dimensions.

Southern geography, characters, and moral values seem exotic in this context. The pages of Faulkner and

*From Tocqueville's *Democracy in America*

O'Connor are drenched with violent or genteel racism, religiosity leading to murder and self-immolation, consciousness unable to escape from crippling family and social narratives, desperate poverty, and enduring ignorance—all of which are digressions from the official American journey.

To immerse myself in my new literary culture, I read two Southern road trip novels. Walker Percy's *The Moviegoer* and Michael Malone's *Handling Sin* portray a spectrum of human dilemmas and emotions: the dread of existential introspection; the intersection of historical consciousness and genealogy; and moments on the journey in which mortality and farce tease us into thought. Now and then such moments intersect, as when we realize that Malone's hero, Raleigh Whittier Hayes, a life insurance salesman, has not spent much time meditating on mortality. As he takes his picaresque journey from a small town in the Piedmont of North Carolina to New Orleans, we follow various plot lines and themes (sins of the father, flirting with the criminal underclass, middle class mediocrity, and the burden of Southern history) as they weave around each other like instrumental lines in a jazz band. In a marvelous stroke, the various plot strands and characters ultimately join forces in the hero's father's actual jazz band.

Malone's novel traces a meandering journey, although with a finite goal of meeting the father, having acquired a few significant pieces of family and Southern history along the way. The road trip follows Sherman's march in reverse, during which we are often treated to parallels with *Don Quixote*—parodic chapter titles, adventures at an inn, encounters with local criminals—except that our hero is not an impoverished aristocrat immersed in literature that imprisons him in a romantic past, and his fat accomplice does not provide a practical counterpoint on his adventures.

In one hilarious episode, our hero, his half-brother, and a few members of the criminal drug trade tromp on Stone Mountain, the Lost Cause's sculptural celebration of Stonewall Jackson, Robert E. Lee, and Jefferson Davis (I like to think of this episode as a comic counterpart to Hitchcock's *North by Northwest*). Until the novel's climax, Hayes is a troubled but mediocre Oedipus, proud of his rational powers and the last to figure out the family intrigue that animates the plot.

Handling Sin's literary ancestors include picaresque novels such as *Don Quixote*, *Tom Jones*, and *A Confederacy of Dunces*. The novel is also a comic version of Flannery O'Connor's more gruesome story "A Good Man is Hard to Find." This Southern Gothic and deeply disturbing tale also includes an unexpected road trip, a view of Stone Mountain, Confederate precious metals, bizarre criminals reminiscent of Faulkner's Popeye, and a disturbing climax with a multi-racial family reunion. It is also reminiscent of Oedipus, in the sense that the journey is made to avoid a family encounter but ends with the very disaster (the massacre of the entire family: father, mother, children, grandmother) it attempted to bypass. Like much of O'Connor, the story takes the trials of Southern religiosity, in which having a personal relationship with Jesus overshadows biblical text or dogma or liturgical ritual, to horrendous extremes.

Southern religiosity is ultimately rejected in Walker Percy's *The Moviegoer*. The hero of this road trip novel, like Raleigh Hayes of *Handling Sin*, is a mediocre middle-class man in the finance industry. But while Raleigh's escape from his socially convenient and comfortable life is engineered by his father, Binx Bolling jumpstarts his own adventure. He is painfully aware that a journey is necessary. "'What is the nature of the search?' you ask. Really it is very simple; at least for a fellow like me. So simple that it is easily overlooked. The search is what anyone would undertake if he were not sunk in the everydayness of his own life." And the journey, in this case through the French Quarter of New Orleans to Chicago and back, begins to free him from the "grip of everydayness." The philosophical journey follows Kierkegaard's path, progressing from the aesthetic level (moviegoing, isolated musing, rejection of family and community, impersonal philandering) to the religious (dogma, sacraments, losing the self in ritual), and finally discovering the ethical mode of being (taking care of a psychologically fragile stepcousin, a relationship in which family and outsiders overlap).

Following Olmsted's footsteps, I took a road trip to the South and felt like a stranger. But ultimately I felt like a stepcousin, part family and part outsider. Struggling on the land, I felt the isolation that accompanies the drudgery and repetition of farm chores. When laborers and trades folk embraced me with generosity and empathy, I felt a redemptive communal spirit. Along the way, the woods and the farm put into high relief thoughts of mortality, and my meagre successes and many failures shocked me into the humble recognition of my insignificance.

Epilogue

*Might He Become a Gentleman Farmer?**

And so, I tried to make the landscape wondrous and the land productive.

For the former I strained my back and studied Olmsted. For the latter I tried to discover what the earth required (such as nitrogen and carbon, native trees, pollinators, local pistils, stamens, and pollen). Although I do much of the work, I am happy to let others plough, sow seeds, take down damaged trees, tend bees, and feed livestock when I cannot.

The talents of real farmers are quantum leaps above my own—they can repair tractors, diagnose animal diseases, determine the pH of soil, boost crops from the ground, and spot where lightning has struck a tree. I operate machinery and hoist sacks of feed hoping not to sever a limb or sprain a muscle. My hope is to retire in the evening with a smile of exhaustion. And I hope not to disappoint Aldo Leopold, who claimed in *A Sand County Almanac* that "the oldest task in human history [is] to live on a piece of land without spoiling it."

I continue to work the land because there is a quiet dignity in digging the dirt. I continue to tend chickens because I can see the pastures come to life with their

*From the "Ithaca" chapter of *Ulysses*

flurry of colors. It turns out that harvesting eggs or buckwheat can turn anxiety into awe. Work can inspire meditation as much as gazing at the beauty of a creek flowing through the woods.

My readings of Thoreau, Darwin, Whitman, and so many others have enriched my experience on the farm. Conversely, as I hope I've shown, farming has helped me understand poems such as "The Red Wheelbarrow" and "The Snake" or parables in the *Gospels* in ways I had not noticed as a student.

I'd like to close these musings with an early poem by one of my favorite poets. Seamus Heaney's ancestors were farmers, and he honored their work in "Digging." I quote the entire poem to invite you to smell the peat and potatoes, and to feel the emotions that bind the generations. The poem miraculously blends the physicality of the land with meditation, a feat I have attempted to emulate:

> Between my finger and my thumb
> The squat pen rests; snug as a gun.
>
> Under my window, a clean rasping sound
> When the spade sinks into gravelly ground:
> My father, digging. I look down
>
> Till his straining rump among the flowerbeds
> Bends low, comes up twenty years away
> Stooping in rhythm through potato drills
> Where he was digging.
>
> The coarse boot nestled on the lug, the shaft
> Against the inside knee was levered firmly.

He rooted out tall tops, buried the bright edge deep
To scatter new potatoes that we picked,
Loving their cool hardness in our hands.

By God, the old man could handle a spade.
Just like his old man.

My grandfather cut more turf in a day
Than any other man on Toner's bog.
Once I carried him milk in a bottle
Corked sloppily with paper. He straightened up
To drink it, then fell to right away
Nicking and slicing neatly, heaving sods
Over his shoulder, going down and down
For the good turf. Digging.

The cold smell of potato mould, the squelch and slap
Of soggy peat, the curt cuts of an edge
Through living roots awaken in my head.
But I've no spade to follow men like them.

Between my finger and my thumb
The squat pen rests.
I'll dig with it.

Heaney compared the grindingly hard work of his ancestors with his writing, a trope that kept him connected to his father and grandfather, insisted on the work ethic of the poet (with admittedly fewer blisters and sore muscles), and kept in memory the value of the earth. My farming ancestors are not genetically my own, but I tread in their footsteps and plant in their fields.

The local folks who have helped me in my amateur pursuits know the earth and the work needed to coax plants and trees out of the ground, and they know how to raise livestock far better than I ever will. Their knowledge has come down from the generations, some since the Civil War, others since the Revolutionary War. Their generosity has made me feel that I share in their ancestry, and I am just as proud of them as Seamus Heaney is of his father and grandfather. I am mad enough to use both kinds of tool, spade and pen, to tend to the land and write at the same time, something Heaney is clever enough to avoid. Even minor signs of success, in the earth or on the page, are due in large part to the grace and wisdom of my neighbors with deep roots in North Carolina soil.

Appendix

Authors and Works Mentioned in the Text

Philosophers

Aristotle, *Metaphysics, Politics,* and *Nicomachean Ethics*
Heraclitus, fragments
James, William, *Psychology*
Lucretius, *On the Nature of Things*
Nietzsche, Friedrich, *Beyond Good and Evil*
Pieper, Josef, *Leisure, the Basis of Culture*
Plato, *Republic*

Landscape Architects

Brown, Lancelot "Capability"
Gilpin, William, *Remarks on Forest Scenery, and Other Woodland Views*
Olmsted, Frederick Law, *Description of a Plan for the Improvement of the Central Park, A Journey in the Seaboard Slave States, Journeys and Explorations in the Cotton Kingdom*
Price, Uvedale, *An Essay on the Picturesque, as Compared with the Sublime and the Beautiful*

Naturalists

Agassiz, Louis, *The Classification of Insects from Embryological Data*
Bartram, William, *Travels*
Berry, Wendell, "The Contrariness of the Mad Farmer"

Darwin, Charles, *Voyage of the Beagle, On the Origin of Species*
Eiseley, Loren, *The Star Thrower*
Haskell, David George, *The Forest Unseen*
Huber, Francis, *New Observations of Bees*
Lawson, *Travels*
Leopold, Aldo, *A Sand County Almanac*
Lewis and Clark, *Journals*
MacDonald, Betty, *The Egg and I*
Rebanks, James, *The Shepherd's Life*
Spence, William, *Introduction to Entomology*
Wohlleben, Peter, *The Hidden Life of Trees*

Southern Writers

Cash, W. J., *Mind of the South*
Clapsaddle, Annette Saunooke, *Even as We Breathe*
Faulkner, William, *Requiem for a Nun, Sanctuary, The Sound and the Fury*
King, Florence, *Southern Ladies and Gentlemen*
Malone, Michael, *Handling Sin*
O'Connor, Flannery, "A View of the Woods," "A Good Man is Hard to Find"
Percy, Walker, *The Moviegoer*
Porter, Katherine Anne, *Pale Horse, Pale Rider*
Ruffin, Thomas, *State v. Mann*
Smith, Lee, *On Agate Hill*
Stephenson, Shelby, *The Hunger of Freedom*, "How We Lived"
Warren, Robert Penn, *A Place To Come To*

Poets

Cohen, Leonard, "Hallelujah"
Dickinson, Emily, "To make a prairie it takes a clover and one bee"
Dillard, Annie, "I Am Trying to Get at Something Utterly Heartbroken"

Eliot, T. S., "Sweeney among the Nightingales"
Gray, Thomas, "Elegy Written in a Country Churchyard"
Hardy, Thomas, "The Farm Woman's Winter," "In Time of 'The Breaking of Nations'"
Heaney, Seamus, "Digging"
Hopkins, Gerard Manley, "Carrion Comfort," "Pied Beauty"
Lawrence, D. H., "Snake"
Mandeville, Bernard, *Fable of the Bees*
Milton, John, "Lycidas," *Paradise Lost*
Mitchell, Joni, "Both Sides Now"
O'Donohue, John, *Anam Cara*
Oliver, Mary, *Upstream*, "When I am Among the Trees"
Plath, Sylvia, "Mushrooms"
Shelley, Percy Bysshe, "Adonais"
Stevens, Wallace, "Anecdote of the Jar"
Williams, William Carlos, "The Red Wheelbarrow"
Wordsworth, William, *Guide through the District of the Lakes in the North of England*
Wright, James "Lying in a Hammock at William Duffy's Farm in Pine Island, Minnesota."
Yeats, William Butler, "Crazy Jane Talks with the Bishop"

Classics

Augustine, *City of God*
Austen, Jane, *Pride and Prejudice, Mansfield Park*
Baldwin, James, "The White Man's Guilt"
Baum, Frank, *The Wizard of Oz*
Bunyan, John, *Pilgrim's Progress*
Carroll, Lewis, *Alice's Adventures in Wonderland*
Cather, Willa, *My Ántonia*
Cato the Rustic, *De Re Rustica*
De Crèvecoeur, Hector St. John, *Letters from an American Farmer*
Dickens, Charles, *David Copperfield*
Doyle, Arthur Conan, "Silver Blaze"
Emerson, Ralph Waldo, "Self-Reliance," "Nature"

Epic of Gilgamesh
Franklin, Ben, *Poor Richard's Almanac, Autobiography*
Genesis
Gospels
Hesiod, *Works and Days*
Homer, *Odyssey, Battle of the Frogs and Mice*
Howells, William Dean, *The Rise of Silas Lapham*
Hurston, Zora Neale, *Their Eyes Were Watching God*
Joyce, James, *Ulysses, Finnegans Wake*
Kazantzakis, Nikos, *The Saviors of God: Spiritual Exercises, The Odyssey: A Modern Sequel*
Petrarch, Francesco, "The Ascent of Mont Ventoux"
Pynchon, Thomas, *Mason & Dixon*, "Entropy"
Smith, Adam, *Wealth of Nations*
Spenser, Edmund, *Faerie Queene*
Steinbeck, John, *Grapes of Wrath*
Thoreau, Henry David, "The Succession of Forest Trees," *Journal*, "Walking," "Autumnal Tints," *A Week on the Concord and Merrimack Rivers, Walden*
Tocqueville, Alexis, de, *Democracy in America*
Tolkien, J.R.R., *The Hobbit, The Two Towers*
Virgil, "Moretum," *Georgics*
White, E. B., *Charlotte's Web, One Man's Meat*
Whitman, Walt, "When Lilacs Last in the Dooryard Bloom'd," "On the Road"

Credits

"Digging" from OPENED GROUND: SELECTED POEMS 1966–1996 by Seamus Heaney. Copyright © 1998 by Seamus Heaney. Reprinted by permission of Farrar, Straus and Giroux. All Rights Reserved.

"Lying in a Hammock at William Duffy's Farm in Pine Island, Minnesota" from COLLECTED POEMS © 1971 by James Wright. Published by Wesleyan University Press. Used with permission.

"To make a prairie it takes a clover and one bee" J 1755/ F1779 by Emily Dickinson. Source THE POEMS OF EMILY DICKINSON, edited by Thomas H. Johnson, Cambridge, Mass.: The Belknap Press of Harvard University, Copyright © 1951, 1955, 1979, 1983 by the President and Fellows of Harvard College.

Harry Kavros is the author of two books, *Dandelions and Honey: Travels on a Forsaken Island* and *Hexameron: A Discussion of Great Books in Six Days*. He is a former dean of Fordham University and Columbia University, where he taught Literature-Humanities (Lit-Hum), the great books seminar. He now lives in Hillsborough, North Carolina.

Printed in the USA
CPSIA information can be obtained
at www.ICGtesting.com
JSHW022230110524
62910JS00001B/2